ECUMENICAL STUDIES IN HISTORY

No. 9

THE CHURCHMANSHIP OF ST. CYPRIAN

by

G. S. M. WALKER

LUTTERWORTH PRESS

LONDON

First published 1968
COPYRIGHT © 1968 LUTTERWORTH PRESS

LUTTERWORTH PRESS
4 Bouverie Street, London, E.C.4

JOHN KNOX PRESS
RICHMOND, VIRGINIA, U.S.A.

7188 1384 7

Printed in Great Britain by
Latimer Trend & Co Ltd, Plymouth

CONTENTS

ECUMENICAL STUDIES IN HISTORY

The purpose of this series is to examine afresh problems of church history, and to do this for the sake of church unity. The subjects are drawn from many periods, places and communions. Their unity lies not in a common outlook of the writers, nor in a common method of treatment. It lies solely in the aim of, in one way or another, directly or indirectly, furthering the unity of the church. The contributors are no less diverse than the subjects, and represent many churches, nations and races.

General Editors

THE REV. A. M. ALLCHIN, Pusey House, Oxford.
PROFESSOR MARTIN E. MARTY, Ph.D., University of Chicago.
THE REV. T. H. L. PARKER, D.D., Oakington Vicarage, Cambridge.

Advisory Board

DR. G. V. BENNETT, New College, Oxford.
PROFESSOR OWEN CHADWICK, Selwyn College, Cambridge.
PRINCIPAL RUSSELL CHANDRAN, United Theological College, Bangalore, S. India.
PROFESSOR HORTON DAVIES, Princeton University, U.S.A.
FATHER B. D. DUPUY, O.P., Catholic Theological Faculty, Le Saulchoir, Paris.
PROFESSOR CHARLES FORMAN, Yale Divinity School, U.S.A.
FATHER BERNARD LEEMING, S.J., Heythrop College, Chipping Norton, England.
PROFESSOR J. D. MCCAUGHEY, Ormond College, Melbourne, Australia.
PROFESSOR JAMES MACEWEN, University of Aberdeen, Scotland.
PROFESSOR JAMES SMYLIE, Union Theological Seminary, Richmond, Virginia, U.S.A.
PROFESSOR RICHARD STAUFFER, Protestant Theological Faculty, Paris.
PROFESSOR BENGT SUNDKLER, Uppsala, Sweden.
PROFESSOR HARRY SAWYERR, University College, Sierra Leone.
PROFESSOR MARTIN SCHMIDT, University of Mainz, Germany.

PREFATORY NOTE

In HIS widely read book on *The Council and Reunion*, Hans Küng appealed to those outside the Roman obedience to consider scriptural and theological arguments for the continuance of a Petrine office in the church. His appeal raises one of the most acute issues in modern ecumenical discussion; some light may be thrown upon it by reviewing our common heritage in early Christianity; and it is in this hope that the following pages on St. Cyprian were written.

I am indebted to the University of Leeds for assistance in publication, and to my colleague, Mr. P. H. Sawyer, for translating some passages from Swedish. To Dr. Northcott and the staff of Lutterworth Press I also owe my grateful thanks.

G.S.M.W.

Department of Theology,
University of Leeds
   All Saints' Day, 1967

NOTE

This book was ready for publication at the time of my husband's death, with the exception of the Index, which has been checked and corrected by his colleague, Mr. H. Willmer, to whom I am most grateful.

M.M.W.

   5th July, 1968

I

CYPRIAN'S BACKGROUND

THE ROMAN provinces of North Africa, that nursery of barristers,[1] bred a religion which had the hardness as well as the clarity of a legal mind. Tertullian, its most brilliant early representative, was able to formulate precise technical terms for Latin theology; Augustine, its later and still more distinguished ornament, stamped the impress of his intellect on much of subsequent Western thought; but both the saint and the heretic added to their mental acumen a moral acerbity which can only be described as puritan. And if the fervour of African Christianity was, in Benson's[2] phrase, "not unlike that with which Ireland has enriched the English bar", it also had the sharp and severe cutting edge of a diamond. For its records[3] begin with the cruel ecstasies of martyrdom, as a stubborn protest against even the best of what was secular; behind it lay the rabbinic legalism of a strong Jewish element, especially at Carthage, which moulded the temper of the first Christians in the locality; around it there flourished a native Phoenician cult of Saturn, whose central act had been the appeasement of an angry god by human sacrifice; and as the church in Africa developed, its language became exclusively Latin, with much Roman influence, and an almost complete absence of the more mellow tones of Greek philosophy.

Few external signs distinguished the African Christian from his pagan neighbour. The linen tunic, dalmatic and cloak[4] which Cyprian wore at his martyrdom formed the common dress of a gentleman at that time. The church buildings were like ordinary houses, except perhaps in having an apse with raised seats for the clergy;[5] and as in other parts of the empire, Christians were known[6] to meet on occasion in their cemeteries. During the third century the size and number of congregations were increasing rapidly, so that by Cyprian's time there must have been about one hundred and fifty[7] bishoprics. Of the bishops' names extremely few are Punic, and only a dozen seem to be non-Latin; hence it may be inferred that at least for its leaders, and probably also in its membership, the church drew heavily on colonial stock. Politically, North Africa was divided into three provinces,

Proconsularis, Numidia and Mauretania, but the church refused to be bound by these divisions. In all his controversies, Cyprian summoned the African episcopate to act together as a united whole, thereby following the conciliar practice of his predecessors, and, although all bishops were theoretically equal, the Bishop of Carthage[8] in fact acted as primate and was popularly known as pope.

This thriving Christian community had enjoyed a long period of prosperity and peace when it was suddenly smitten, about the middle of the third century, by the twin scourge of plague and persecution. A type of malignant typhoid fever, comparable in some respects to that which attacked the Athens of Pericles, broke out in Ethiopia and Egypt during the year 250; by 252 it had reached Carthage and it continued to ravage the empire for a further twenty years. In many minds it inspired an almost morbid meditation of death, but Christians responded with aid to the victims, under the motto of *noblesse oblige*[9] and without discrimination of either race or creed. Meanwhile, the persecution of Decius had touched the weak spots in an unprepared church; along with martyrs there were many apostates; and these lapsed Christians felt so deep a sense of ignominy that in several cities they came near to lynching[10] the bishop whose absolution they had sought in vain.

Among such a people, severe, proud, practical, fervent and at times ferocious, Caecilius Cyprianus[11] was born at an early date[12] in the third century. He belonged to Africa Proconsularis, the most decidedly Roman of the provinces, and seems to have spent his life at Carthage where he practised as an orator and owned a pleasant house with gardens.[13] But the easy, opulent life of a provincial capital began to dissatisfy him, despite the obvious integrity of his somewhat Stoic[14] character. Becoming disillusioned with his former occupation,[15] he turned to a study of the Bible[16] and was then guided into the church by the venerable priest Caecilian. Cyprian's account of his conversion is less personal and vivid than the spiritual autobiography of Augustine, but it describes what is fundamentally the same type of Christian experience.

"After the stain of my former life", he writes,[17] "had been cleansed through the laver of regeneration, and a light from above poured into my heart now purged and pure, after the second birth with its draught of celestial spirit had refashioned me into a new man, then at once my doubts were miraculously resolved, doors opened, darkness became light, and what had formerly seemed difficult turned into an easy task. . . ."

Like Augustine, Cyprian belonged to the twice-born type of religious

8

genius. Like him again, he combined catholic churchmanship with an evangelical experience of grace.

As a result of his conversion, Cyprian took three immediate steps. Although Caecilian his mentor had been a married man, he vowed himself to celibacy, for which his main reasons seem to have been disgust at contemporary sexual ethics[18] coupled with a belief in the world's decline[19] and approaching end. In the second place he sold his property[20] for the benefit of the poor, retaining or otherwise receiving back a portion which he subsequently administered[21] as bishop, and throughout his Christian life he showed a marked concern for social welfare. In the third place, renouncing secular studies, he confined his reading for the future to the Bible and Tertullian.

The break with his classical past was not in fact complete, for although his works contain no citations of pagan literature, rhetorical training still coloured his pure Latinity; and according to a reliable tradition[22] he had perfected the ancient system of shorthand known as Tironian Notes, by means of which he was able to record with great accuracy the views of the eighty-seven bishops[23] who attended his council on rebaptism in 256. It is, however, true that "he carried out with much more consistency than Jerome"[24] his self-denying ordinance against the pagan classics, a fact which must be borne in mind when tracing the sources of his particular ideas.

A man of Cyprian's background and ability was bound to be treated from the outset as an eminent member of the church. None the less it was surprisingly quick promotion when he became a bishop after having been a Christian for no more than two or three years. The date of his conversion is not precisely known, but it probably took place in 245[25] or 246;[26] his consecration as bishop must be dated[27] not earlier than June 248 nor later than April 15 (Easter Day) 249. From the start of his episcopate he had to face the opposition of disgruntled rival candidates, but although he had not himself desired office, he belonged, like Ambrose, to the ruling classes and demanded obedience with the imperious tenacity of a Roman magistrate. Within a matter of months the Decian persecution had been launched, to be continued with intermissions by that Emperor and his successors until Cyprian's death by martyrdom in 258.

The conflicts and trials of the period are reflected in a series of letters and treatises[28] which show the high ideals and sometimes unpractical conclusions of an intensely dedicated mind. Ardent love for his flock forms the keynote of all that Cyprian did and wrote.

9

"My very dear brothers", he told[29] his people, "I suffer pain in not being able to come to you in person at this moment . . . constant sorrow and groaning . . . tears which flow day and night, because the bishop whom you elected with such love and ardour has not yet been permitted to greet you and hold to your embrace."

But if the bishop was bound to the flock which had chosen him as pastor, he felt an even closer tie to God from whom his appointment ultimately derived. For Cyprian, as for Ignatius before him, the episcopate is a supernatural gift or charisma which places its holder under divine inspiration and control. Not only his preaching but also his administrative actions are inspired of God. Cyprian often receives special revelations which direct his conduct.[30] He has to ask his Lord whether he can grant absolution to an individual, and enjoys frequent dreams and visions which his opponents think absurd.[31] And he concludes a letter to Pope Cornelius with the words:[32]

> The Lord, who deigns to choose and institute bishops in his church protects them once chosen and instituted by his will and assistance, controlling them through inspiration (*gubernanter inspirans*) and supporting them not only with strength to restrain the contumacy of the wicked but also with mildness to encourage the repentance of those who fall.

Early in his episcopate[33] he compiled a treatise in three volumes called the *Testimonia*. This was a collection of biblical passages used in catechesis, with an amplitude of quotation and a skill of arrangement which make it an outstanding example of the genre.[34] The attitude is one of deep reverence for scripture, but the method of using detached proof-texts does not indicate a very profound approach. Several characteristic themes make their appearance—a marked sacramental emphasis, abhorrence of schism and respect for the clergy, a long section on moral conduct, appeal to prophecy and the guidance of the Spirit—but in one respect the work shows traces of its early date among his writings: Cyprian makes no reference to priesthood in the Christian church, and when he mentions the priest of the new sacrifice[35] he thinks of Christ alone.

If Cyprian's piety was nourished on the Bible, he interpreted it by the light of his personal experience, and in terms of his constant study[36] of Tertullian. Thus, his beloved concept[37] of the church as mother doubtless had a biblical basis, although the classic text in Gal. 4: 26 is never quoted in his writings. It has been plausibly connected[38] with the new birth which he had himself experienced at his conversion. But above all it was derived from Tertullian, who makes an exceptionally[39] frequent use of the idea. Tertullian finds it by implication in the doctrine of the Trinity, since the names Father and Son suggest the existence of a mother;[40] it is in the house of a mother that the newly baptized spread out their hands in prayer for the first time with their brethren;[41] and "our lady mother the church" cares for the imprisoned martyrs.[42] Further, God knew that man was to benefit from the sex of Mary and thereafter of the church,[43] for Christ's sleep in death resembled the sleep of Adam in that from his wounded side the church was shown forth as the true Eve or mother of the living.[44]

While there can be no doubt of Cyprian's constant dependence on Tertullian, verbal parallels[45] are not numerous and the influence is shown in thought content rather than in literary style.[46] Thus, when Cyprian says[47] that heresies and schisms are of recent birth, abandoning the head and source of truth, he borrows a leading idea from Tertullian's *De praescriptione hereticorum*; but a subtle change from legalism to mysticism is effected by the more ecclesiastical context in which the Bishop of Carthage writes. One of his earliest productions as a Christian, the little treatise *Quod idola dii non sint*, makes use of Tertullian's Apology in its closing section and its ninth chapter[48] is inspired by the same author's *De testimonio animae*.

It has already been noted that Tertullian links his doctrine of the church with his doctrine of the Trinity. The same point can be illustrated from a number of metaphors which are carefully repeated by his disciple. *Matrix* is a term employed by Cyprian to denote the church as the womb or source of spiritual life. Thus, converted heretics return to the *veritas* and *matrix*, and travellers to Rome must recognize the true church from schismatic bodies by attaching themselves to the *matrix* and root of catholicity;[49] above all, those who separate from the *matrix* cannot live and breathe apart, but lose the substance of salvation.[50] The same term is applied by Tertullian both to God and to the church, when describing the original source of divine life and apostolic truth. Of God he writes:[51]

When a ray proceeds from the sun it is a portion from the whole, but because it is the sun's ray the sun will remain in it, and the substance is not separated but extended, as light kindled from light. The *matrix* of a substance remains whole and unimpaired, even if you derive from it several offshoots of its quality; in the same way, what emerges from God is God and the Son of God and both are one, and again in the same way, Spirit from Spirit, God from God, has made a numerical distinction of degree and not of essence, being different in measure and proceeding but not separating from the *matrix*.

Of the church he writes[52] that the apostolic preaching can only be verified from churches of apostolic foundation, and he continues:

> If this is so, we must at once agree on the truth of all doctrine which conforms to those churches, the apostolic *matrices* and originals of the faith, since it indubitably holds what the churches received from the apostles, the apostles from Christ, and Christ from God.

Since Tertullian thus traces a succession running back through the apostles to God, he can readily describe the divine unity by a term which is also applicable to the church's fountainhead. Ecclesiology is expressed in the language of theology because the life of the church is a real extension of the life of God. Cyprian equally regards the church's unity in charity as a terrestrial image of the triune being of the Godhead writing[53] of "this unity which descends from the divine consistency and co-inheres with celestial mysteries . . . which if a man does not preserve, he loses life". In consequence he can transfer directly to the church a series of similitudes which Tertullian had employed in definition of the Trinity. In a well-known passage[54] Tertullian expands his earlier picture of a ray of sunlight by adding those of the stem from a root and of the river flowing from a spring (*solis radius, radicis frutex, ontis fluvius*) to express distinction of persons in unity of substance:

> For God emitted his Word, according to what the Paraclete also teaches, as the root sends forth a stem, the spring a river, and the sun a ray . . . every source is a parent (*omnis origo parens est*) and everything which proceeds from the source is an offspring . . . and yet the stem is not separate from the root, nor the river from the spring, nor the ray from the sun . . . nothing is divorced from the *matrix* from which it draws its peculiar attributes.

Cyprian takes[55] the same three similitudes, makes a slight change of language (*solis multi radii, rami arboris multi, de fonte uno rivi plurimi*), and uses them to illustrate the relation between the one church and its many local congregations:

> The church is one but extends broadly into a multitude by increase of fertility, just as the sun has many rays but one light, a tree has many branches but one strength drawn from the clinging root, and while many streams flow from the spring . . . unity is preserved in the source (*unitas tamen servatur in origine*), . . . there is one head, one source, one mother abundant in fertile issue.

If Cyprian figures above all as the apostle of church unity, it should be remembered that he based his doctrine on what Tertullian had taught him of the unity of God. From this it follows that, although the apostles preached throughout the world and founded churches in every city, yet there is only one apostolic church of which each local cell is an offshoot; and Tertullian finds[56] the proof of their unity in the practice of inter-communion, brotherhood and mutual hospitality, governed by the single tradition of one and the same sacrament.

"There is only one baptism for us", he writes,[57] "according to both the Lord's gospel and the apostles' letters, since there is one God and one baptism and one church in the heavenlies . . . but heretics have no share in our discipline, and the very absence of communion indicates that they are foreign . . . since they do not have the same God as us, nor one and the same Christ, and therefore not one baptism because it is not the same—when they do not have it lawfully, they doubtless do not have it at all."

Cyprian's denial of the validity of baptism ministered outside the church, which was to provide the occasion of his major conflict and to bring on him the anger of the Pope, was directly derived from the teaching on the one church which he had found in Tertullian.

Ecclesiastical unity must have a point of origin, since the apostolic church is founded on the apostles. Tertullian pertinently asks[58] heretical sects to indicate the source of their existence, and if they wish to link themselves with the apostolic age, to show an episcopal succession deriving its authority from some apostolic figure at the beginning of the line. When he wrote in these terms Tertullian was still a catholic, expressing the traditional orthodox apologetic, and after becoming a Montanist he would have placed more reliance on unmediated contact with the Spirit. But it is worth dwelling on this side of his theology because of its importance for the thought of Cyprian.

Both of the African writers employ the term *cathedra* to describe an apostolic see. Whereas Irenaeus, who anticipates their appeal to episcopal succession, prefers to speak of bishops occupying the place[59] of the apostles, Tertullian advises[60] his reader to scan those churches where the very chairs of the apostles (*cathedrae apostolorum*) still preside in their localities, and Cyprian[61] makes pointed if perplexing use of the phrase *cathedra Petri*. Both had attended the rhetorical schools in which the teacher occupied a chair, and thus there may be some pagan background to the term; but one may surmise that it originated at Rome, where Hermas[62] had beheld the church as an aged lady sitting on a

13

throne and the Muratorian fragment had described Bishop Pius as occupying the *cathedra* of the Roman Church.

To a Christian of North Africa Rome was bound to appear eminently apostolic, but Tertullian does not connect its status exclusively with Peter.

"If you are close to Italy", he writes,[63] "you have Rome whence for us also authority is near at hand. How happy is that church on which the apostles poured their whole doctrine along with their own blood, where Peter imitates the Lord's Passion and Paul is crowned with the same death as John."

In addition to Paul's emulation of the Baptist, he refers to the Apostle John being plunged at Rome into burning oil and subsequently banished, and continues by mentioning the doctrinal unanimity which extends to the African churches. Peter stands with the other apostles at the source of this authority, and the church's unity is in fact symbolized by his position.

"Only Peter", Tertullian writes,[64] "I find from the mention of his mother-in-law to have been a married man, but I assume him to have been the husband of one wife for the sake of the church which, built upon him, was to appoint every rank of its ministry from among monogamists."

As the Rock, Peter received the love-token of a peculiar name,[65] derived from the biblical typology of Christ as the chief corner-stone; and it should further be remembered[66] that it was through Peter, who first received them, that the Lord bequeathed to the church the keys of heaven. However, when Maccarone contends[67] that such language implies an office over the church universal, it must be added that Tertullian nowhere regards Peter as the sole and unique holder of such an office.

Writing the *De praescriptione* in his catholic days, he had joined Paul and John with Peter as witnesses to the apostolicity of Rome. Later, as a Montanist, he extended the apostolic gift to include all spirit-filled Christians, and accused catholics of confining to the institutional church what belongs of right to each disciple of the Paraclete. The passage[68] is so significant for Tertullian's ecclesiology that it deserves a fairly full quotation:

I am now investigating your (catholic) opinion and the reason why you usurp this right for the church. If it is because the Lord said to Peter, On this rock I will build my church, I have given you the keys of the heavenly kingdom, or, Whatever you bind or loose on earth will be bound or loosed in heaven, do you therefore claim that the power of loosing and binding has

also descended to yourself, that is[69] to every church related to Peter? Who are
you to overthrow and alter the Lord's clear intention of bestowing this gift
on Peter personally? He says I will build my church on you and I will give
the keys to you, not to the church, and, Whatever you loose or bind, not
what they may loose or bind. . . . In Peter himself, that is to say through him,
the church has been built and it is he who handled the key . . . finally he was
the first to open the gate of the heavenly kingdom by Christian baptism . . .
thus the power of loosing and binding transferred to Peter had no reference
to the mortal sins of those who already were believers[70] . . . what then has
this to do with any church, and particularly with yours who are unspiritual?
For in view of Peter's person that power will suit spiritual men whether they
be apostle or prophet. Indeed the very church is properly and originally[71] the
Spirit himself . . . and in this sense the church will certainly forgive sins, but
it will be the church of the Spirit acting through a spiritual man, and not the
church considered as an aggregate of bishops. For right and judgment belong
to the Lord and not the servant, to God himself and not a priest.

Despite its authorship, this passage does not represent the extravagant
ravings of a nonconformist.

Origen[72] gives a similar if more restrained exegesis of the Petrine
texts, remarking that the promise of the keys was given "to Peter and
to every Peter", so that bishops are justified in using it as a basis for
their claims, provided that their conduct is similar to that which first
deserved the promise; and in criticism of a uniquely Petrine prerogative he asks the question, "But if you think that the whole church is
built on Peter by himself alone, what have you to say of John and each
of the apostles?"

To Cyprian, the visible church with its organization meant more than
it did to Origen;[73] but what is remarkable in Tertullian's account is the
way in which he combines a symbolic unity with a practical multiplicity. Notwithstanding his refusal to see in the Bishop of Rome, or
indeed in any member of the episcopate, a continuing prerogative of
office, he none the less attaches to Peter's person an immense significance for the structure of the church. At the outset Peter was the
church, it was built upon him, and without him it could not have
come into existence; yet his primacy means nothing more than a temporal priority, and his successors are not the holders of his office but
those who share his spirit.

Cyprian adapted much of Tertullian's argument in expounding
what he meant by the Petrine primacy, but he was able to apply it
within an institutional conception of the church, because he regarded
the episcopate as a charisma and thus identified bishops with Tertullian's

spiritual men. In order that this identification should be plausible, the bishop had to be endowed with the Spirit—if he fell from grace he ceased to be a bishop—and thus the agreement between Tertullian and Cyprian is even closer than might at first appear. Both writers regard ambition and disobedience as the main cause of schism;[74] both object[75] to the title *episcopus episcoporum* as presumptuous; and both use a form of conciliarism[76] to express the corporate nature of the church.

Since authority thus depends on a spiritual charisma, whether it be of office or of personal endowment, a continuing presence of the Spirit is essential to the church's existence. Tertullian the catholic[77] quoted Pentecost as its scriptural foundation, asking heretics who rejected the Book of Acts on what ground they could claim either a mission of the Spirit or the status of a church. Tertullian the Montanist[78] was so anxious to emphasize the church's spiritual nature that he interpreted I Cor. 5: 5 to mean that the sinner must be excommunicated in order that the *church's* spirit may be saved.

It is at this point that he differs from the thought of Cyprian. Where the latter relied on sacramental grace and the inspiration of the clergy, Tertullian came more and more to teach the priesthood of all believers. In his catholic days[79] he had accused the sects of interchanging clerical and lay functions:

> Today a presbyter, tomorrow a layman, for even on the laity sacerdotal duties are imposed.

Yet even at this early date, while insisting on differences of rank he had none the less believed in a universal priesthood.

> "We", he wrote,[80] "are the true worshippers and the true priests, who pray in the Spirit and sacrifice our prayer in the Spirit as God's fitting and acceptable victim."

And so he had not changed his fundamental outlook when, in a Montanist work of later date,[81] he declared that second marriages are no more permissible for laity than clergy, since laymen too are priests (*sacerdotes*); that the difference between ordained and unordained is one of purely ecclesiastical arrangement; and that where there is no constituted bench of clergy, any Christian offers and baptizes and is a priest for himself alone.

Hence arose a minor difference of terminology. By Tertullian[82] the bishop is described as "high priest" since every member of his flock has a sacerdotal character and he is the leader of a priestly people. By Cyprian, who may well be following a Roman tradition at this point,[83] a human high priest is never mentioned and in his developed conception of the church the bishop is the one and only priest.

While Tertullian distrusts[84] an indiscriminate exercise of the priestly power of absolution, he has such confidence in spiritual gifts that he would prefer an inspired layman to an official pope. One of his most revealing passages[85] describes the dear sister who received charismatic revelations during divine service. When the Spirit came upon her in ecstasy, she conversed with angels or even with the Lord, saw and heard mystic secrets, discerned men's hearts and issued prescriptions for the sick. Her revelations tended to substantiate the views of preachers whose teaching she approved; and thus, while Tertullian himself was discoursing about the corporeal nature of the soul, she beheld a spirit in bodily or substantial form, God and the apostle being both invoked to sponsor her veracity.

This account, however lurid and fanatical it may appear, is not entirely remote from the spiritual experience of Cyprian. He also[86] saw visions and dreamt dreams which guided him by direct communication with Christ; but in his case, and this is the distinctive feature, it was as a bishop that he received these gifts. Indeed, his official status may explain the one case in which he departed seriously from the moral teaching of his predecessor. Tertullian had entirely disapproved of flight in persecution, but he made an exception[87] for the peculiar circumstances of the apostles, to whom alone he thought that the instructions of Matt. 10: 23 applied. Did Cyprian justify his own flight because, in the circumstances peculiar to the third century, he identified[88] apostles with bishops? His flight was certainly not due to cowardice and he agreed with Tertullian[89] on the supreme bliss of martyrdom. In Cyprian's view, which here expresses the quintessence of African Christianity, spiritual charisma and sacerdotal character are both manifested to the full when the bishop offers himself in imitation of the Passion of his Lord.

"C'est jusque dans le martyre", as Colson[90] well puts it, "que le grand evêque de Carthage incarnera cet idéal."

But Cyprian believed that the martyr no less than the charismatic must be integrated into the corporate life of the Christian institution. He was determined[91] to suffer in his episcopal city, surrounded by his own flock, in the dual role of God's spokesman to them and of their representative at the court of heaven. One is inevitably reminded of the attitude expressed by the great martyr-bishops of the second century,

Ignatius of Antioch and Polycarp of Smyrna. During his lifetime, Cyprian had encouraged by letter those who suffered for the name of Christ; after death, his memory continued to inspire the martyrs, as in the case of the little priest Marianus[92] who, after horrible tortures, dreamt that the Bishop of Carthage appeared at the right hand of the divine Judge to strengthen him and lead him forward.

Thus Cyprian's biography written by Pontius became a model for subsequent saints' lives. And whenever she sings her *Te Deum*, the church quotes Cyprian, for it was his pen[93] which first described the glorious choir of the apostles, the band of triumphant prophets and the innumerable host of martyrs.

In preparation for the world's imminent end and final judgement, he believed that the church must be disciplined for the fight with Anti-Christ as an army under her appointed bishops. But stalwart churchman as he was, he appreciated the immense spiritual power which Montanism had attempted to embody. He sought to harness that power within the confines of institutional religion, and to combine two antithetic concepts of the church[94] through the medium of what can best be described as prophetic catholicity.[95] Too often the institution falls short of the ideal; frail earthen vessels are unable to contain the fervour of the Spirit; and the tension between priest and prophet reaches breaking point. Starting from an exalted pattern for the episcopate, Cyprian developed a false doctrine of the sacraments, because he confused personal spirituality with official status; seeking to promote sanctity among his colleagues, he came to deny the indelibility of orders and the objectivity of sacramental grace. But if the Donatists were justified in appealing to one aspect of his doctrine, their sectarianism was the direct opposite[96] of all that he held dear. And although in practice it may seem rent by contradictions, his teaching on the church and still more his love of unity retain an ecumenical significance. Seventy years ago, Benson[97] wrote words which still deserve attention:

> He was tempted into the noble and alas! too fruitful error of arraying the visible church in attributes of the Church Invisible. But he said and showed how men might gravely dissent without one wound to peace. He spoke a watch-word of comprehension which, for lack of the charity which possessed him, we do not receive in the churches, although it must needs precede the Unity we dream of.

II

THE PRIORITY OF PETER

WHEN HANS KÜNG, in a moving and important book,[1] described the search of Roman Catholic theologians for a theory of the Petrine office which would be obviously relevant to modern conditions, he made several statements bearing a connexion with the thought of Cyprian:

> The essential point is that the relation of bishops to Pope corresponds to the biblical relation of Apostles to Peter. We must curtail neither the rights of the Petrine office (which is conciliarism) nor the rights of the apostolic office (which is papalism) . . . from the beginning the church has had *two* principles of unity: the bond between the bishops and the see of Peter, and the bond *between the bishops themselves.*

Cyprian would not have employed precisely these expressions, and indeed it is doubtful whether he would have understood "the See of Peter" as referring exclusively to Rome; but it is no anachronism to ascribe to him a juxtaposition of similar ideas, whose paradoxical nature has led very different schools of thought to combine in quoting his authority. Towards the close of the first Vatican Council,[2] one speaker appealed to Cyprian in support of papal infallibility; on the other hand, Hugo Koch[3] states bluntly that Cyprian of Carthage is an episcopalian from head to foot, and a more recent writer[4] complains that the saint does not seem to have grasped with any clarity the place of Peter and his successors at Rome within the structure of the church universal. Perhaps he suffered what Küng has elsewhere[5] called "the irony of fate" when he saw what he had regarded as the centre of unity becoming an occasion of schism. One must not expect an entirely consistent theology in a writer who had little training or experience, and throughout his short career was to some extent feeling for his way. It is true that Cyprian sometimes contradicted himself, and that his arguments on occasion could be "opportunist in character";[6] but once the misunderstandings have been removed, a reasonably clear and coherent scheme of thought emerges.

Cyprian's principal contribution to the subject formed the very first

19

treatise ever to be written on church unity. Its title as known to the Reformers was *De simplicitate praelatorum*, an untranslatable phrase which means that in each local congregation there can only be one bishop; for this there is some early manuscript support, coupled with the evidence of Fulgentius[7] in the sixth century. The title now universally accepted, *De catholicae ecclesiae unitate*, would have the same import in Cyprian's mind, for to him the unity of the church is intimately connected with the one episcopate.

Schism, being a sin against charity, is utterly unchristian, and those who separate from the church are beyond the sphere of grace. Such is the main burden of the treatise; but the date when it was written is so vexed a question that the particular schism which it envisages is far from clear. Monceaux[8] compares the first chapter, where Cyprian warns that a delusive peace might prove as dangerous as actual persecution, with the opening of the *De lapsis* which also speaks of peace being restored to the church; he concludes that both were composed in the spring of 251, after the Decian persecution had for the moment ended; and he refers to a letter[9] written subsequently in the same year, which explains that both treatises had been read publicly at Carthage, copies of them being enclosed for perusal by the confessors at Rome.

Two schisms faced the church in 251, that of Felicissimus in Africa and the one which Novatian engineered in Rome a little later; the traditional view was that Cyprian directed his *De unitate* against both. Benson,[10] however, listed seven passages where he detected allusions to Novatian's assumption of the bishopric, and he found none relating to the African schism; he therefore inferred that Cyprian read his treatise to the council meeting in the spring of 251, after the affair of Felicissimus had been disposed of and before the conduct of Novatian was discussed. But as Chapman[11] argues, this would imply that the entire treatise was written within a matter of hours, between the arrival of Pompeius with Stephanus from Rome and the final conciliar decision; he considers it more reasonable to suppose that Cyprian wrote it earlier, during the leisure of his retreat, in which case it must have referred exclusively to the African schismatics. Koch and Caspar[12] agree with this conclusion, but Koch spoils the force of his argument by listing several passages[13] which mention the rivalry of a pseudo-bishop, and since the party of Felicissimus did not possess one until 252, these references can only envisage Novatian. Bévenot[14] believes that the Roman rebel had tried to get recognition at Carthage before Cyprian wrote his treatise, and he is therefore not in favour of the earlier date.

THE PRIORITY OF PETER

The most plausible solution is that suggested[15] by Dom J. le Moyne. No passage, except possibly the conclusion of the third chapter, need refer to Felicissimus, but at least two, as Koch had noted, must be directed against Novatian; the treatise was therefore written about the middle of 251, and cannot have been read to the council of bishops which assembled in the spring. However, it was Cyprian's regular practice[15a] to have important documents read to a congregational meeting of his flock at Carthage, and it was to this and not to an episcopal council that his account of a public reading referred.

The problem is further complicated by the existence of two separate versions of the treatise. There are minor differences in the nineteenth chapter, but the main divergence occurs in chapters four and five. One version, known as the Primacy Text (PT) because it states that a *primatus* was bestowed on Peter, was first published in 1563; the other is known as the Textus Receptus (TR) since it had been received as standard prior to that date. In order to clarify the position, which has a direct bearing on Cyprian's concept of the Petrine office, the versions will be shown in parallel columns after the introduction which is common to both.[16]

(cap. 4) . . . the Lord speaks to Peter, saying I declare to you that you are Peter and on this rock I will build my church and the gates of hell will not overcome it. I will give to you the keys of the kingdom of heaven, and what you may bind on earth will be also bound in heaven, and whatever you may loose on earth will be also loosed in heaven (Matt. 16: 18 sq.).

PT	TR
I. And he also said to him after his resurrection, Feed my sheep (John 21: 17).	
II. On him he builds the church and entrusts him with the sheep to pasture,	II. He builds the church on one,
III. and although he assigns a similar power to all the apostles, yet he established one chair and arranged by his authority the source and structure of unity.	III. and although after his resurrection he assigns a similar power to all the apostles, saying, As the Father sent me I also send you, Receive the Holy Spirit, If you remit the sins of any they will be remitted to him, if you retain those of any they will be retained (John 20: 21-23), yet in order that he might display a unity, he arranged by his authority the source of the same unity originating from one man.

21

PT	TR
IV. The remainder were indeed what Peter was, but a priority (*primatus*) is given to Peter, and one church and one chair (*cathedra una*) are displayed;	IV. The remaining apostles were indeed what Peter was, endowed with a similar share of honour and of power, but the beginning arises out of unity in order that the church of Christ may be displayed as one.
V. and all are pastors, but one flock is shown, which is shepherded by all the apostles with unanimous assent.	V. And this one church is also depicted in the Song of Songs by the Holy Spirit speaking in the person of the Lord, My dove, my unblemished, is one, she is the only one for her mother, the chosen of her parent (Song 6: 8; English versions 6: 9).
VI. If a man does not maintain this unity of Peter, does he believe himself to maintain the faith?	VI. If a man does not maintain this unity of the church, does he believe himself to maintain the faith?
VII. If he deserts the chair of Peter, on whom the church was founded, does he trust that he is in the church?	VII. If he rebels and resists the church, does he trust that he is in the church, when the blessed apostle Paul also teaches the same and shows the sacrament of unity, saying, There is one body and one Spirit, one hope of your calling, one Lord, one faith, one baptism, one God (Eph. 4: 4–6)?
(cap. 5)	VIII (cap. 5). This unity should be maintained and appropriated with firmness, especially by us bishops who preside in the church, so that we may prove the episcopate itself to be one and undivided.
	IX. Let none deceive the brotherhood by lying, let none defile the truth of faith with treacherous prevarication.

The episcopate is one, part of which is held in totality (*in solidum*) by each. The church is one, but extends broadly into a multitude by increase of fertility. . . .

At first sight, and for several centuries after its publication, the Primacy Text appeared to be strongly papalist in tone. Applying the phrase *cathedra Petri* exclusively to Rome, Benson[17] declared that it "admittedly must be from the pen of one who taught the cardinal doctrine of the Roman See", and the learned Anglican archbishop proceeded to castigate the sins of the papistical forger of this document. Since he knew it only in a text conflated with TR he was able to dismiss it as a series of tendentious interpolations, a hostile attitude which had already been taken by Hartel in his edition of the works of Cyprian.

But the problem was placed in a completely new light by Dom Chapman's[18] discovery of manuscript evidence for PT as an independent entity; it could no longer be a matter of interpolation, but of alternative versions, both of which Chapman considered to be genuine; and he produced reasons for thinking that TR had been written first and with reference to the local situation at Carthage, while PT followed as a subsequent revision directed against the Novatianist schism at Rome.

His views were accepted by Harnack and a number[19] of distinguished scholars. Batiffol and Lacey[20] agreed in accepting the authenticity of PT, but they regarded it as the original version with a purely Roman reference, TR following later so as to give the treatise wider application. But Koch[21] devoted his great patristic knowledge to maintaining the spurious character of PT, which he sought to prove on grounds of literary style no less than of theology, and in this he was supported by a few[22] conservatives.

None of those who accepted both versions had found a convincing reason for the writing of a second, until van den Eynde[23] argued with great acumen that Cyprian had been obliged to modify an original PT during the baptismal controversy, when his Roman opponents gave it a more papalist interpretation than he had intended it to bear. This view has subsequently held its ground, being accepted not only by Chapman himself but also by Bévenot and the majority[24] of critics.

There are, however, a few diehards who still adhere to a single version. Ludwig[25] considered that PT was alone authentic, TR having been composed by one of Cyprian's supporters during the dispute on baptism, with a slight but obvious change in literary style and rhythm. On the other hand, le Moyne[26] argued for the sole authenticity of TR; he suggested that PT had been composed after Cyprian's death by a clever stylist, who copied his language to express a different doctrine of the Roman See; he compared its standpoint with the school of Optatus of Milevis, and thought that it originated in Africa, perhaps in opposition to the Donatists.

This long debate has produced a number of ironical results. For over three centuries TR was supposed to have been interpolated by a papalist forger in favour of the Roman primacy, but detailed study of the manuscripts has now shown[27] that in the conflated version PT was actually interpolated from TR. Further, and even more surprising, we now find the Benedictine Dom le Moyne championing that attack on PT which had previously been sponsored by protestant opponents of the papacy. In reality, the theological argument is inconclusive, for there is nothing in PT which Cyprian could not have written but much[28] that a papalist would have tended to omit. And the fact that TR has better manuscript support can be explained either on the ground that it was original, or that Cyprian meant it as a later definitive edition to suppress its predecessor.

Study of the work as literature suggests a more positive conclusion. Ludwig[29] was quite correct in pointing to linguistic parallels with the letter of Firmilian, which suggest that Pope Stephen had been claiming a primacy in phrases reminiscent of PT; and he was also right in saying[30] that the rhythm and assonance of PT have been broken in TR, which indicates that the former is the earlier version. It fits into the rest of the chapter with a lean but firm consistency of thought, whereas TR is by contrast an expanded muddle of irregularly connected ideas.

Bévenot's section I with its quotation from the fourth gospel follows logically after the scriptural citations in the text common to both versions; it leads on to the discussion of the one pastoral office which occupies sections II to V; separation from this one office is shown in sections VI and VII to involve both a denial of the faith and schism against the church; and from this the common text resumes logically[31] with its statement that both episcopate and church are one.

But TR loses the connexion with what precedes by dropping the whole of section I and the Petrine reference of section II; section III is amplified by a scriptural quotation on the equality of the apostles which breaks into the sequence of the argument; section IV omits the *primatus* of Peter, substituting a much vaguer phrase ("the beginning arises out of unity") whose meaning can only be interpreted by turning back to PT; section V is entirely replaced by another scriptural quotation, which illustrates the unity of the church but drops the unity of the pastoral office; the same result follows, in sections VI and VII, from the replacement of Peter by the church and the addition of three Pauline verses; and in consequence two new sections (VIII and IX) have to be created, with a forced mention of "us bishops", in order to link with the "one episcopate" with which the common text resumes.

One might possibly surmise that IX is an oblique criticism of Stephen, whose "treacherous prevarication" had misinterpreted Cyprian's original PT in terms of a papal primacy. TR is a rambling and confused revision of a passage which had previously been short and clear; its muddle and bulk are caused by omitting all but one of the references to Peter and by adding three fairly long quotations from the Bible.

These three, as van den Eynde[32] has shown, are never used by Cyprian prior to the baptismal controversy, although between the spring of 251 and that of 254 he wrote at least six treatises and some thirty-one letters; to this must be added the fact, also noted by van den Eynde, that what he elsewhere says about the Petrine position agrees with PT prior to 255 and with TR thereafter.

The conclusion that PT was the original version is reinforced by a technical problem[33] in chapter nineteen of the treatise. Here manuscripts containing the PT of chapter four, as Chapman had already noticed without finding the correct explanation, read *hic* in reference to the schismatic and *ille* in reference to the lapsed,[34] whereas in the manuscripts of TR these two words are reversed. The reading of PT would suit the year 251, when the schismatics were under immediate consideration and the lapsed, having just been dealt with in the treatise *De lapsis*, were of more remote concern. And the date can be fixed with even greater precision by Bévenot's discovery that some, though not all, of the PT manuscripts read "those who have sacrificed" in place of "the lapsed". Now we know that the council of 251 admitted to communion all the apostates, except for those who had committed the extreme sin of offering pagan sacrifice, and even these were absolved by the council of 252 in view of a fresh threat of persecution. It follows that the *sacrificati* were only doing penance as a class by themselves during the period 251 to 252, and therefore that PT was written during the same chronological limits. No explanation is offered of why TR should have inverted the words *hic* and *ille*; but it may be suggested that at a leisurely revision the grammatical context was seen to be improved by such a change.

The question whether or not TR was written by Cyprian is unimportant for the present purpose; if not, its author was certainly a supporter who expressed his ideas in a somewhat weakened form. However, it is of great significance to establish Cyprian's authorship of PT, coupled with the fact that if he wrote two versions this was the original, because it thus embodies his first reflections, uninhibited by any later controversy, on the relation of Peter to the church. In order to clarify his ideas, it will be necessary to concentrate on two difficult conceptions, the *primatus* and the *cathedra Petri*.

A great deal of confusion has been caused by translating the word *primatus* as "primacy" and assuming that it has the same meaning in Cyprian as it would bear today. From the whole tenor of Cyprian's writings it is obvious that he meant nothing of the kind.

How then is the word to be translated? He twice[35] gives it a non-classical usage in the plural to express the right of primogeniture which Esau forfeited. In the singular it occurs in the Latin of Col. 1: 18 which he quotes[36] without comment, except in so far as it forms part of a series of texts illustrating the primogeniture of Christ. When describing the Novatianists, he says[37] that by dividing the church and rebelling against the peace and unity of Christ they try to set up an episcopal chair for themselves and assume a *primatus* and claim the power to baptize and offer. It is possible[38] that the word here signifies the first rank among the local clergy; but as the schism is compared in the same passage to the intrusion of Korah and his companions into the priesthood, and as Novatian's own sin was that he intruded into a see which already had a catholic bishop, it may equally be that his assumption of a *primatus* means a claim to be the first occupant of the see since it fell vacant, on the ground that his rival, though consecrated earlier, had an invalid title.

The meaning is much more certain in the passage[39] where Cyprian describes the argument between Paul and Peter (cf. Gal. 2: 11 *sq.*), saying that the latter made no insolent claims or arrogant assumptions by insisting that he held the *primatus*; this is to be interpreted in the light of the immediately preceding statement that the Lord chose Peter first (*primum*), and of that which immediately follows designating his rivals as newcomers and juniors (*novellis et posteris*). In other words, when Cyprian ascribes a *primatus* to Peter—and he is the earliest writer so to do—he means that Peter was the first of the apostles to be chosen; his "primacy" is a priority in time[40] and not a supremacy of jurisdiction.

That this is also the meaning of the term in the Primacy Text of *De unitate* chapter four, is shown by the fact that the paraphrase offered in the Textus Receptus reads "the beginning arises out of unity". Peter was the senior apostle with all—but no more than all—that that implies, and Poschmann[41] ascribes too much to his position when he calls him the source of all ecclesiastical authority. Chronologically this is true; but since the Primacy Text itself insists on the equality of the apostles, it cannot mean that they were subject to Peter's power.

None the less, Cyprian accepts wholeheartedly the biblical teaching that the church was built upon Peter. The letter[42] which describes his

26

argument with Paul—that episode which was to become a standard protestant argument against the papacy—says that the Lord chose Peter first and built the church upon him. Another letter,[43] which equally dates from after the baptismal controversy and therefore cannot be interpreted in a papalist sense, repeats without embarrassment the same Petrine foundation:

> Where is a thirsty man to go, to the heretics where the fountain and stream of living water is entirely absent, or to the church which is one and is founded by the Lord's voice on that one who also received its keys?

What Cyprian understood by this is best explained in the light of the second chapter[44] of De unitate. Those who follow in Christ's footsteps are there compared to the house founded on rock (super petram) which does not fall; all Christians must therefore follow Christ's words, teaching and doing exactly what he taught and did, since it is impossible to have faith without keeping the commandments. In other words, the foundations of the Christian life are obedience and faith, the precise virtues which are attributed to Peter. As Cyprian elsewhere[45] puts it, he on whom the church was built spoke with the church's voice as one on behalf of all when he asked, Lord to whom shall we go? thou hast the word of life eternal. And Christ entrusted the sheep to his pastoral care, placing and founding the church upon him, when he like his Lord had neither gold nor silver.[46] Peter is in fact the foundation of the church because his example is the source and grand original of obedient faith.

The power of absolution granted first to him[47] was later bestowed on all of the apostles, but the building on one man illustrates and declares the origin of unity; and this structural source of church unity in Peter [48] is parallel to the one baptism and the one Spirit whose ministrations are confined to the one church. But just as the apostolate of Peter, originally unique, expanded into a college of twelve, so his one pastoral office is perpetuated in a multitude of bishops, all of whom share in his prerogatives provided that they display his loyalty and faith.

> "When our Lord", writes Cyprian,[49] "whose precepts we must fear and preserve, was arranging both the honour due to a bishop and the structure of his church, he spoke in the gospel saying to Peter, I say to you that you are Peter and on this rock I will build my church. . . . From this, carried on by temporal successions, the ordination of bishops and the structure of the church descends, in such a way that the church is constituted upon the bishops and her every action is controlled through the same leaders."

The episcopate continues the Petrine office, which is not located exclusively at Rome, and each bishop is to his own flock what Peter originally was to the first disciples; but although one and the same pastoral office is thus transmitted from one generation to another, remaining central to the church's unitary structure, the *primatus*, in the sense of temporal priority in which Cyprian understood it, must be attributed to Peter personally and to him alone.

From this it follows that the "chair of Peter" is to be found in each orthodox bishopric, since all of the Petrine position that could be inherited by his successors is shared equally by the whole episcopate. As Bévenot[50] puts it, the *cathedra Petri*

> is perpetuated in all sees the bishops of which have been legitimately appointed, and their legitimacy is established by the recognition of those already sharing in that *cathedra*.

This is clearly the meaning of the phrase in the Primacy Text of *De unitate* chapter four, since it is immediately followed by a mention of the one episcopate which is jointly held by all the local incumbents. At Carthage it was held by Cyprian, and thus Optatus,[51] writing a century later and with stronger Roman sympathies, says that it was not Caecilian but Majorinus who seceded from the chair of Peter/Cyprian. The same usage continued even in the sixth century, when Gildas[52] complained that unworthy bishops were usurping Peter's chair in Britain.

There was, of course, a double sense in which the Roman bishop could be said to occupy that chair; he not only held a share in the one pastoral office, but he held it in the locality where it had been exercised by Peter. Thus Peter's place (*locus Petri*) is in general terms no more than the rank of an episcopal throne (*gradus cathedrae sacerdotalis*), but in the Roman context[53] it becomes successively the place of Fabian and of Cornelius. In the one other passage[54] where Cyprian uses the phrase, he refers primarily but not perhaps exclusively to the Roman See. He says that Felicissimus and his fellow-schismatics, having set up for themselves a pseudo-bishop, are venturing to sail to Peter's chair and to the principal church, the location of which is specified a little later by mention of the Romans; now there are a number of instances[55] in Cyprian's Latinity where the conjunction *atque* is used to link a term of general reference with one of more specific denotation, and the passage could therefore be interpreted as meaning that they sail not only to an orthodox bishopric (*Petri cathedram*) but in fact and more specifically to Rome. Firmilian of Caesarea[56] also uses the phrase, but with a sarcastic

28

tone which implies that Pope Stephen, being infected by a communion with heretics which destroys the truth of the Christian rock (*petrae*), cannot validly claim to possess through a mere succession the Petrine chair (*Petri*). It thus appears that any see, including the Roman, can forfeit this title if it deserts the apostolic faith.

However, even if Peter's chair is occupied jointly by all the orthodox episcopate, there is none the less a manner in which the Roman Church enjoys as Peter did the pre-eminence of a temporal priority. Cyprian writes, in a passage[57] already quoted in part, that supporters of the African schismatic Felicissimus

> venture to sail and carry letters to Peter's chair and to the principal church from which the episcopal unity arose (*ad ecclesiam principalem unde unitas sacerdotalis exorta est*) . . . and do not consider that these are Romans whose faith was praised in the apostle's preaching. . . . For when . . . to individual pastors there is assigned a portion of the flock, which each rules and governs in such a way that he will render account of his action to the Lord, it is certainly the duty (of Christians) . . . to refrain from gadding about and disrupting the concord of the bishops.

Here the equal authority of bishops and the unity of the one pastoral office are stressed from start to finish; but just as the college of apostles had its origin in the calling of one man, so the Western family of churches has a common source in one church, which by the preaching and residence of Peter has been located at Rome.[58] This is the *ecclesia principalis* out of which the one episcopate expands.

Koch[59] has indeed argued that *principalis* is to be interpreted as *principis* and *unde* to be taken with *Petri*, so that the phrase would be translated "to the chair of Peter and church of the chief apostle from *whom* the episcopal unity arose"; but although this is grammatically possible, it does not suit the context which has a Roman rather than a Petrine reference, and at the same time it gives to Peter's chair a more decidedly local application than Cyprian's usage elsewhere would allow.

The Bishop of Carthage never describes Peter as "prince" (*princeps*) of the apostles, but only as *primus* among equals. Similarly, looking from a Western standpoint, he regards Rome as first among the churches, because it was the earliest to be founded in the West and from it the whole Christian mission originated. Poschmann[60] translates *ecclesia principalis* as *Urkirche*, possessing a chronological priority but no supremacy of jurisdiction, and this interpretation can be illustrated from examples of both classical and patristic Latin.[61] Benson[62] thinks of the Augustan conception of the principate when he describes Rome, in

Cyprian's mind, as "first and highest in a great Republic of churches, securing administrative unity and freedom".

But although the authority of Rome must not be exaggerated,[63] its unique position among the churches must equally not be minimized. There are passages in Cyprian's correspondence where he identifies catholic unity with the Roman communion. Thus he writes[64] that he has been persuading all his colleagues to hold communion with Cornelius because that is to be equated with the church's unity, and in similar vein he tells[65] the African bishop Antonian that to communicate with Cornelius is to communicate with the catholic church. Now the background to these letters is the Novatianist schism, during which the catholic church at Rome was represented by the party of Cornelius; Koch[66] is correct in maintaining that Cyprian's remarks merely mean that catholics elsewhere should communicate with the catholics at Rome; and since Cornelius is the lawful bishop it would be a breach of unity if other churches were to recognize his rival. On the other hand, a disputed election to some minor see would be comparatively unimportant, whereas "rival bishops at Rome", as Chapman[67] rightly notices, "would divide the church and to communicate with the wrong one would be schism".

The special status which the Roman Church derived from its priority is well illustrated by the case involving Marcian of Arles. This prelate had seceded from catholic unity by joining the Novatianists[68] and in order to preserve an orthodox church at Arles it was necessary to obtain the appointment of a successor. Faustinus of Lyons, the local metropolitan, was unable to intervene effectively and asked for help from Rome; failing to obtain it he wrote to Cyprian, who instructed Pope Stephen to make the new appointment.

To put it in these words is no exaggeration of the ambivalent attitude which Cyprian shows toward Rome. On the one hand, he writes in magisterial tones, virtually commanding the Pope to do his duty; on the other, he assumes that a mere word from Stephen will put all the affairs of a distant church in order. Even Koch admits[69] that there the Roman See exercised a moral eminence. When the local episcopate was powerless, and when Cyprian's high standing proved of no avail, the Bishop of Rome had only to write a letter of nomination "by which another may be substituted" in the schismatic's place.

If, however, Rome fails to do her duty, Cyprian's attitude changes from respect to opposition. This change appears to some extent in the earlier case of the Spanish appeal, and it becomes even more pronounced over the validity of extra-ecclesiastical baptism. In Spain, two apostate bishops had been deposed by the local episcopate and reinstated on appeal to Rome. When the Spanish churches asked Cyprian to reverse the papal judgement, he did so in a council of thirty-seven bishops which met under his presidency at Carthage in A.D. 254, and without troubling to make any reference to Rome, he forthwith notified[70] this conciliar verdict to the clergy and people of the two bishoprics involved. Stephen may have been misinformed on the fact of the accuseds' apostasy, but to Cyprian the case is completely clear: God rejects apostates from among the clergy, as can be proved from scripture, and we must therefore obey God rather than the Pope. As Benson remarks,[71] such conduct is compatible with the idea of Rome as the senior church and centre of unity, but not with that of Rome as a centre of jurisdiction or even of appeal.

When Stephen insisted on the validity of schismatic baptism, provided that the correct form and matter had been used, he touched a particularly painful nerve in the spiritual anatomy of Cyprian. The Roman practice seems originally to have been universal, and it was only under Agrippinus of Carthage[72] in the early third century that the African church had begun to rebaptize its converts. But Tertullian had approved of this, and still more it seemed a logical consequence of Cyprian's belief in one church as the sole vehicle of grace. For him to accept that baptism could be validly ministered in schism would have been tantamount to admitting that the church could be divided and still remain the church.

In opposing Pope Stephen on this issue, he obtained the support of Firmilian and other Eastern bishops who, in a council at Iconium[73] not earlier than A.D. 230, had agreed in voting for rebaptism. Cyprian conceded[74] that in the former days of ignorance, when schismatics had been accepted into church membership as if they were baptized, God had granted them a special grace to cover the deficiency of the church's practice. But with the fuller understanding which Cyprian believed himself to have acquired, it would have been a sin against God and a failure in duty to the converts, if they had not been given the grace of catholic baptism on entering the church.

He obtained the votes of eighty-six other African bishops[75] in support of his opinion, and when Stephen persisted in condemning it, the next logical step would have been for Cyprian to excommunicate the Pope. But he never even considered such action, for at the back of his mind always lay the idea that catholic unity could only be preserved in communion with Rome; and all that he did was to claim the right for independent judgement, declaring[76] that none of the Africans would set himself up as a bishop of bishops to compel the obedience of his colleagues by the terrorization of a tyrant.

In practice, Cyprian continued to have a deeper respect for Rome[77] than his strict theory of the church should have permitted. He probably revised the Primacy Text of *De unitate* so as to avoid a papalist misinterpretation during the baptismal controversy, and whenever he thought the Pope to be in error he refused to submit to his authority, maintaining that every bishop has an equal right of personal decision. But at the same time he realized that the church universal required a permanent centre of gravity at Rome, just as each local church needed one central figure in the person of its bishop.

However vehement his criticism, he never dreamt of breaking off communion with the Roman See, for to do so would have been to sever himself from the church's origin, and even in the midst of disagreement unity must be preserved. The Pope was not, in Cyprian's view, infallible and his decisions could be reversed by a subsequent council, as happened with the Spanish appeal; but the papacy possessed such immense executive authority, and its position appeared so central to the church's structure, that without it the church would be dismembered.

Such ideas were never fully formulated by Cyprian even to himself, but they underlie the profound deference with which his letters are addressed to Rome.

III

THE COLLEGIALITY OF BISHOPS

IF PETER and the Eleven formed a nucleus or prototype of the church in miniature, the same structural formation was repeated as the body of believers grew; each bishop occupies the place of Peter within his own locality, and the episcopate as a whole constitutes an apostolic college in which every member has an equal right. But according to Cyprian, the Petrine position was not perpetuated with reference to the church universal, since only the local congregation has a single head on earth. In the beginning there had been no more than one congregation, with Peter chronologically pre-eminent; as congregations multiplied, each came to possess a Peter in the person of its own bishop; but they remain a spiritually united group of separately independent cells, and there can be no super-church with a "super-Peter" at its head.

This is why Cyprian[1] so firmly follows Tertullian in denying that there can be any "bishop of bishops" of the character to which later Popes laid claim. It is immaterial whether he was directly attacking Stephen[2] in this statement. Even if he were merely curbing the pretensions of a local African episcopate, he laid down a principle by which papalism was explicitly rejected. The only head of the universal church is Christ, whose judgement must be awaited in case of disagreement; meanwhile every bishop has a personal authority and complete freedom of action, so that he can neither judge nor be judged by any other. Cyprian gives concise expression to these ideas when he says that the bishop is responsible to God alone.

But ironically enough it was from Rome, as Bévenot[3] has demonstrated, that he derived this concept of direct responsibility to God. During the Decian persecution he wrote to the Roman clergy to explain the reasons why he had gone into hiding, and they replied[4] by saying that, although a good conscience is usually content with God alone as judge (*solo Deo iudice esse contentus*), yet Cyprian is worthy of double praise for submitting his actions to the approbation of his brethren, and they are sure that he applies to them in the character of participants rather than of judges.

33

This letter dates from the vacancy after Fabian's martyrdom, and it was penned by Novatian who was at the time an orthodox presbyter of the Roman Church. He meant no more than to pay Cyprian the usual courtesies of an epistolary *captatio benevolentiae*; but in the early years of his episcopate the Bishop of Carthage attached immense value to any document emanating from Rome, and he turned what had been intended as a piece of politeness into a point of principle.

No previous Christian writer had said that God alone is the judge of episcopal conduct, and in practice Cyprian regularly notified Rome[5] of all his major problems and decisions. But he kept Novatian's letter beside him, and by 252 he was using its principles to condemn[6] the schism of Novatian himself; since every bishop must render an account of his own decisions to the Lord, it is ridiculous for him to excommunicate other bishops over a matter of discipline. An identical point is made in other letters[7] of the same year, when Cyprian maintains that in governing his portion of the flock the individual pastor must give an account of his actions to the Lord, and declares that those who refuse absolution to penitent apostates will have to render a reason in the day of judgement.

The same phrases recur yet again in the literature[8] of the baptismal controversy, during which Cyprian fought for the bishop's right of private judgement as a vital issue. This is part of the reason why he never dreamt of excommunicating Stephen, despite his violent disagreement with that Pope; if the Roman bishop had no authority to judge the Africans, they were equally unqualified to pass judgement upon him. Similarly when a local bishop erred in the administration of penance, Cyprian's council[9] noted his mistake but declined to reverse his decision, and when another bishop asked his colleagues to discipline a contumelious deacon, Cyprian[10] in praising his humility pointed out that he could well have acted on his own initiative.

But this episcopal independence was not quite unlimited, since the very status of a bishop depended on recognition by his colleagues and if he lost their communion, as happened when the Bishop of Arles became a Novatianist,[11] he lost at the same time all legitimate authority. If the collective episcopate could not pass judgement on any of its individual members, it could always turn a bishop into a layman simply by expelling him from the episcopal college.

Such elaboration illustrates one aspect of development in the doctrine of the ministry which had taken place by Cyprian's time. It can be argued that the embryonic organization portrayed in the New

Testament embodies various trends, which may be distinguished as congregational, presbyterian, episcopal and, in a limited sense, papal. It is certainly true that the first clear account of monarchical episcopacy is found in Ignatius of Antioch, and that the Ignatian bishop, being pastor of a single congregation, is unlike any bishop known as such today.

Cyprian's system of church order has been compared by Lacey[12] and others to that of Scottish Presbyterianism, with its congregational meeting, session of presbyters or elders, and single pastor in charge of each locality. Some Scottish parishes are at least as large as was Augustine's flock at Hippo, and since many African bishoprics were very small, Cyprian's bishop is more parochial than diocesan in stature. So far at least the comparison is valid. But Cyprian's councils had less authority over their members than is possessed by a Scottish General Assembly, because his doctrine of episcopal independence, in the context of numerous diminutive sees, really made him a congregationalist rather than a presbyterian. In this respect he had not advanced far beyond the congregational episcopacy of Ignatius; his bishop is still the pastor of a single congregation, able to delegate much of his work to presbyters in an emergency, but in normal circumstances functioning as the sole minister of word and sacraments to all his people.

However, in developing a theology of the episcopate[13] Cyprian went farther than his predecessors. To Ignatius the bishop appeared primarily as a defence against schism, and by Irenaeus he was regarded as the guardian of doctrines received by succession from the apostles. Cyprian combined the two ideas so that the church was made to depend on the apostolic succession of its bishops. He did not place the ministry within the body of the faithful, nor can he really be said to have placed it above them, in view of his insistence on popular election and on the people's right to reject a heretical or otherwise unworthy pastor; rather it seems that the bishop is prior to his congregation, in the same way as Peter was prior to the church. If this episcopal priority be granted, Cyprian gives a high status to the members of his flock, the *populus Christianus* or *genus divinum* entered by the second birth of baptism, in which all as children of God are brothers and remain so after death.

None the less he ascribes to the Christian ministry an authority which may well be modelled on both Jewish and Roman precedents. As a member of the empire's ruling class he naturally thought of his office in terms of a Roman magistracy,[14] using the legal language of *honos, munus, officium, administratio* and so forth. But this was an unconscious usage, and whenever he quotes his sources they are always taken from the Old Testament. It is God's will that a priest (*sacerdos*, by which term he regularly means a bishop) should be chosen in the presence of all the people, just as Moses was instructed by God to place Aaron and Eleazar in front of the whole synagogue,[15] so that those who knew the candidates personally might be able to declare the merits or defects of each. Apostate clergy must be unfrocked because the priests of the old dispensation had to be unblemished,[16] and there is a reiterated[17] quotation of Deut. 17: 12–13 to reinforce the necessity of obedience to the priesthood.

Cyprian took the Mosaic law literally, making frequent use of it in his *Testimonia*, and he believed that the Christian ministry inherited from its Jewish predecessor a right to maintenance from the people's gifts. He followed Clement of Rome[18] in equating bishops with Old Testament priests, but made presbyters and not deacons the equivalent of Levites. Similar ideas are found in Tertullian who, however, accompanied them with an explicit doctrine of the priesthood of all believers. The latter doctrine was never stated by Cyprian, although he was careful to associate the people with him in all his major decisions, and he defined[19] the church as consisting in bishop, clergy and the faithful.

He was thus[20] neither papalist nor exclusively episcopalian in his doctrine of the church; but he took a rather idealistic view of episcopacy because of his belief in its divine institution; and although he allowed that an individual bishop might fall into error, he thought the collective episcopate to be infallible on condition that it was governed by the Holy Spirit and abode in Christ.

All of the clerical orders are mentioned[21] by Cyprian with the exception of doorkeepers (*ostiarii*) who are found[22] in the contemporary church at Rome. Presbyters can celebrate[23] in the bishop's absence and may also deputize for him at font, pulpit and confessional; they often distribute alms,[24] and there is a distinct class of teachers knows as *presbyteri doctores*;[25] the *presbyterium* is the group forming the bishop's council, but during a vacancy[26] they have little independent power. Deacons are always mentioned after presbyters,[27] whose place they can take to minister absolution[28] in cases of emergency, but their special functions are to serve the bishop in administrative and charitable work[29] and to assist the celebrant whether he be presbyter[30] or bishop. To discipline junior clerics,[31] who can no more rebel against his authority than he can against God's, the bishop may withhold their monthly allow-

36

ance pending a full investigation in the presence of clergy and people. Although Cyprian accepts and uses a diversity of clerical orders, for him the essential ministry is that of the episcopate. As the regular celebrant of baptism, confirmation and eucharist[32] the bishop occupies a *cathedra* and *primatus* among the other clergy. Certain sees, in particular those of Rome, Carthage and Lyons, appear to have an administrative pre-eminence, but in theory all bishops hold an equal share in the one episcopal office. Each owes his appointment to the approval (*iudicium*) of his neighbouring colleagues, following the attestation (*testimonium*) of clergy and assent (*suffragium*) of people. The episcopate expresses its unity through the action of provincial councils and synodical correspondence, but at the local level no congregation can have more than a single bishop since the existence of two would divide the church. If the bishop is in the church, the church is still more in the bishop[33] because he is its foundation and embodiment, and his powers are so directly derived from God that Cyprian can write,[34]

We by divine permission water God's thirsty people and guard the confines of the living springs.

Occupying so exalted a position, his example is of great importance to the flock,[35] he should not engage in secular business,[36] and those who have weakened under persecution[37] are ineligible for the episcopate. If he stands firm like Zacharias[38] the priest of God may be slain but cannot be overcome, and it behoves him[39] to confess and suffer in his own city.

The titles used by Cyprian to describe a bishop include *praepositus* (prelate) and *antistes* (president), but the most common term is *sacerdos* (priest). This usage is undoubtedly derived from the parallel, first drawn in detail by Clement of Rome, between the Jewish priesthood and the Christian ministry, but it does not appear in Cyprian's early work, the *Testimonia*, where[40] Christ is regarded as the Christian priest. However, he soon forgot any hesitation which he may have felt in employing sacerdotal language, and became the first author to make what Lightfoot[41] has called the "transition from the universal sacerdotalism of the New Testament to the particular sacerdotalism of a later age".

In doing this he was not entirely innovating,[42] for similar language is adumbrated in Tertullian and Origen; but Cyprian gave it an exclusive emphasis which was really and radically new. Whereas the old idea was that all Christians are priests and their sacrifices are common prayer, he restricted[43] priesthood to bishops and sacrifice to celebration of the eucharist; moreover, as Harnack[44] writes, he was not only "the first to associate the specific offering, i.e. the Lord's Supper, with the specific priesthood", but he was also "the first to designate the *passio Domini*, nay the *sanguis Christi* and the *dominica hostia*, as the object of the eucharistic offering", when he stated[45] that "the passion of the Lord is the sacrifice we offer".

In so far as presbyters can celebrate in the bishop's absence, they also can be entitled priests; but Watson[46] notes that "in Cyprian's writings there is no passage where *sacerdos* must, and not many where it can, be equivalent to presbyter". His more usual expression is to say[47] that presbyters are "joined with the bishop in sacerdotal honour". But fulness of priesthood is possessed only by the bishop; the *collegium sacerdotale*[48] is the collective episcopate, and when Cornelius became bishop he had already "been promoted through all the ecclesiastical offices"[49] before "he mounted to the lofty pinnacle of the *sacerdotium*".

If Cyprian represents a largely new departure for the doctrine of the ministry, his doctrine of the sacraments is also new in part. In the administration of baptism he indeed followed the practice of his predecessors, even when it differed from that of Rome, but whereas his friend Firmilian[50] argued that persons baptized outside the church could in no case have a higher status than that of catechumens, Cyprian[51] allowed that if such people had formerly been admitted to communicant membership, God would supply them non-sacramentally with the grace of baptism. He refused[52] to draw a literal parallel between baptism and circumcision by enjoining that infants should be baptized only on the eighth day after birth, and instead he treated the eighth day as a typological prophecy of the resurrection. He distinguished[53] between baptism and confirmation respectively as sacramental regeneration of water and of the Spirit, believing that the Spirit is bestowed on the baptized through imposition of the bishop's hand.

On the eucharist, however, he conflated several trends of thought which had previously been held in isolation. Justin Martyr,[54] for example, regarded Christ's body and blood as food for the Christian soul, and he also referred to the "pure offering" prophesied by Malachi, but Cyprian with his emphasis on a sacrificial priesthood refused to keep the two conceptions separate.

It is one thing to say, as did earlier writers, that the eucharist is a sacrifice of thanksgiving to God and also to say that it is the body and blood of Christ on which we feed. It is altogether another thing to put them together, as

Cyprian does, and to say that in the eucharist we offer the body and blood of Christ as our sacrifice.[55] (*milan*)

Such language could envisage a repetition of Calvary by the human priest, although here it remained "so to speak only a notion verging on that idea",[56] and it is impossible to estimate how far it represents a survival of paganism in Cyprian's understanding of sacrifice and priesthood; such ideas were entering into the atmosphere of the third-century church, but he probably imagined that he was doing no more than summarize his predecessors' thought. It might well be true to say that, in the tradition[57] of Ignatius and Polycarp, he regarded a bishop's martyrdom as the supreme example of pontifical high mass. But it is more obvious and certain that he was concerned above all to secure exact obedience to the dominical institution of the sacrament.

His statement[58] that "the passion of the Lord is the sacrifice we offer" is made in opposition to the *hydroparastatae*, those ancient teetotallers who used water without wine in the communion chalice. Certain ignorant or simple bishops, he says, have failed to imitate the actions of "our Lord and God Jesus Christ, the author and teacher of this sacrament", who used a mixed chalice and called the wine his blood, so that if wine is absent Christ's blood is not offered, nor is the dominical sacrifice validly consecrated if it does not correspond to his passion.

For if Christ Jesus our Lord and God is himself the high priest of God the Father, and offered himself to the Father in sacrifice, and taught this to be done for his remembrance, then doubtless his place is truly taken by that priest who imitates what Christ did, and a true and perfect sacrifice is then offered in church to God the Father, if he begins to offer according to the observed manner of Christ's own offering.

Whether or not Cyprian drew the conclusion when he penned these words in the year 253, their implication is not difficult to trace; if the bishop is to complete a real *imitatio Christi*, he must sooner or later be a martyr.

Besides the invalidity caused by a failure to follow Christ's institution, communion could also be ministered unlawfully if the church's discipline was not observed. One almost overhears a Scottish "fencing of the tables" when Cyprian writes[59] that, since St. Paul has warned against the danger of communicating unworthily, the Lord's body is profaned by those presbyters who admit to communion before the completion of penitence and pardon. The eucharistic elements have a double significance because the body of Christ, sacramentally present on the altar, is also found mystically in the church.

> For inasmuch as Christ bore all of us, having borne our sins, we see that water represents the people and wine reveals the blood of Christ. But when water is mixed with wine in the chalice, the people is united to Christ and the faithful are assimilated and joined to him in whom they have believed. This assimilation and union of water and wine is so commingled in the Lord's chalice that the commingling cannot experience a subsequent separation. . . . And by this very sacrament the unity of our people is revealed, so that just as many grains make one loaf when gathered and ground and mingled into one, we may likewise know that we are one body in Christ who is the bread of heaven. . . . [60]

It would thus be impossible for Cyprian to have tolerated communion in one kind; on the contrary,[61] the soldiers of Christ, awaiting the onset of persecution, should daily drink the chalice of Christ's blood in order that they may be fortified to shed their own blood for him. The confessors in prison[62] are regularly communicated by visiting clergy, and on the anniversary of martyrdoms[63] the eucharist is celebrated for the martyrs' repose. But if a cleric accepts the office of trustee contrary to episcopal regulations, Cyprian forbids[64] a requiem to be offered after his decease. Rich members should bring gifts for the poor to the sacrament, and it is doubtful[65] whether their communion is valid if they fail to do so. Excommunicates who receive unworthily are punished by fearsome prodigies, such as[66] the vomiting which assailed a little girl after her nurse had taken her to a pagan sacrifice, the fire bursting out of a box in which an apostate had attempted to reserve the sacrament, and the sword, poison or cinder into which it turned on their approach.

As the minister of such awe-inspiring mysteries, the bishop must be surrounded by an aura of divine right. It is "God who makes bishops"[67] in the same way as bishops make deacons. The people are indeed responsible for seeing that a suitable candidate is chosen, but he is not their delegate, and their vote only manifests "the judgement of God"[68] from whom the episcopate comes as a direct charge in token of the divine charity uniting the members of the church. In the Old Testament those who disobeyed the priest were executed; under the new covenant bishops wield the spiritual sword of excommunication, which inflicts a spiritual death since outside the church[69] there is neither salvation, grace nor life. Cyprian lays even more stress on the bishop's authority than on his preaching or sacramental functions, and as Bernard[70] remarks, "it is rather as rulers of the church than as its teachers that Cyprian conceives of himself and of his brethren in the episcopate". But in exercising this authority the bishop must at all times have the support and approval of his colleagues, and if he forfeits this he ceases to possess his own share in the one episcopal office.

Notorious misconduct as in the case of the two Spanish bishops, or open schism as perpetrated by Marcian of Arles, is regarded by Cyprian as evidence of a divine judgement already passed against the offending prelate,[71] and the faithful are justified in withdrawing from his communion, although the sentence is not definitive until the episcopal college has approved the appointment of a successor. Indeed the people (*plebs*) of the local congregation, who "chiefly have the power of electing worthy priests or rejecting the unworthy",[72] commit a grave sin if they remain in communion with a sacrilegious bishop. Hosea 9: 4 provides a warning against such contamination, and Moses instructed the people to separate from the tabernacle of unhallowed priests.

It will be observed that Cyprian will not allow that the eucharist can truly be consecrated, so that the faithful are profited thereby, if the minister be an unworthy or heretical bishop. That is to say, he has no thought of the indelible character of the priesthood; nor does he distinguish between *invalid* ministrations and those which are only *irregular*.[73]

However discrepant these views may be from a later orthodoxy, he believed them to be based on scripture and implied in the unity and sanctity of the apostolic church.

Not only must the bishop maintain the purity of apostolic doctrine. As a successor of the apostles[74] he must maintain the divinely given unity which they have handed down, to ensure that mother church does not lose her wandering and bleating (*balabundas*) lambs. His actions must be entirely guided[75] by the dominical source and apostolic tradition from which his own order originates. There is thus only one lawful line of succession in the ministry, and if a pretended bishop intrudes into a see which is not vacant, his consecration is invalid and he remains a layman.

"If the church was to be found with Cornelius", writes Cyprian[76] in reference to the Roman schism, "who succeeded to Bishop Fabian by a legitimate ordination, and whom the Lord glorified by martyrdom in addition to the honour of priesthood, then Novatian is not in the church nor can he be counted as a bishop, since in contempt of evangelical and apostolic tradition he succeeded no one but originated from himself. A church cannot be held or maintained by him who was not ordained within the church."

41

Novatian had in fact been consecrated by the imposition of episcopal hands, but this was null and void since it took place in schism; "it was not merely that he lacked jurisdiction, he lacked the character, the orders of a bishop";[77] and as there is no church outside the line of legitimate succession, so no one can be a bishop if he does not succeed to a vacant see.

It is thus that at the local level the unity of the one episcopal office is maintained. Cyprian[78] owes his own episcopate both to the suffrage of his people and to the judgement of God. The proper and almost universal[79] procedure at episcopal elections is that the neighbouring bishops of the same province should assemble, and the new bishop be chosen in presence of the flock which best knows the life and character of each. After election he notifies[80] other members of the episcopate by letter, so that their approval may admit him to membership of the "sacerdotal college", and if there is a disputed election they must decide between the rivals.

Such a dispute occurred in the case of Cornelius, the validity of whose position Cyprian[81] recognizes for the following reasons: he was supported by the judgement of God who made him bishop and by the concordant testimony of the universal episcopate, he was not suddenly promoted but had advanced through all the ecclesiastical orders, he neither sought nor desired a bishopric in the manner of some proud and headstrong candidates but had to be compelled to accept office, he was consecrated by many of Cyprian's colleagues with the judgement of God and Christ, with the testimony of almost all the clergy and the suffrage of the people then present, and he was appointed to a vacancy in the place of Fabian/Peter and the rank of the sacerdotal throne.

In all this the divine will, expressed through the church's action, is the decisive factor. Lawful bishops are made by a decree of God[82] or divine ordination,[83] and since the church is one as God is, the appearance of a second bishop in the same see,[84] setting up another church and dividing Christ's members, would contradict divine appointment, evangelical law and catholic unity.

With this verdict Cornelius[85] was in entire agreement when he wrote that "there ought to be one bishop in a catholic church". The day of suffragans or co-adjutors had not yet dawned, for the flock was still small enough to have a single pastor; and the sin of the Carthaginian rebel Felicissimus[86] was that "in trying to break the people into pieces he separated sheep from shepherd, divided sons from their father and disjoined the members of Christ".

Since the one bishop is so intimately associated with the one church, Cyprian in writing to a church usually addresses its bishop alone. He writes to his brother Cornelius or his brother Jubaianus as the case may be. During a vacancy he addresses the clergy (*Cyprianus presbyteris et diaconis Romae consistentibus*) or the clergy and people, and when separated from his own flock he adopts the same address. But in normal circumstances he identifies[87] church and bishop, so that *ecclesia* and *episcopus* become synonymous terms, the unity of the catholic church is correlated with the college of the joint episcopate, and rebellion against the bishop means secession from the church.

Colson[88] recognizes this fundamental point when he remarks that "église et évêque sont deux termes interchangeables sous la plume de saint Cyprien", and Strotmann[89] puts the same point differently when he describes the bishop as the localization of catholicity for his flock. Theologians of the Eastern Orthodox communion would be ready to agree that the bishop is the bond between his local church and the church universal.

Since there is only one episcopate, founded on Christ's promise to Peter, each bishop occupies the *cathedra Petri* as regards his own flock, but is at the same time a member of the world-wide episcopal college. Indeed, the episcopate is the great organ of church unity[90] which is maintained, in Cyprian's vivid phrase,[91] "by the glue of priests in mutual concord". "For although we pastors are many" he writes[92] to Pope Stephen, "yet we feed one flock, and we must gather and cherish all the sheep whom Christ sought with his blood and passion". Though each has an administrative independence and personal responsibility, all bear each others' burdens through conciliar action and correspondence, and Peter is not only the centre of the local congregation grouped around one bishop, but also the bond of the church universal in the one episcopate.

In order that this unity should be manifested, it is essential for all bishops to be inspired and controlled by the same Holy Spirit; a bishop who breaks the concord of his brethren must at once be rejected from their fellowship; "for there can be no difference of opinion among us in whom one Spirit dwells, and if we observe anyone to disagree, it is obvious that he does not retain the Holy Spirit's truth with the remainder".[93]

At the head of the local congregation, the bishop is the focus of a brotherhood whose members are united to Christ and to one another through him; the union of the presbytery around its bishop is symbolic

43

of sharing in a common rule, a common faith and a common love; administration and discipline are expressions of this single purpose, which reaches its sacramental climax in the eucharist.

But the practical defect in Cyprian's high doctrine of the ministry is that it breaks into fragments if there is a genuine and honest disagreement which bishops push to the extreme of mutual excommunication.

During an episcopal vacancy the local presbyters and deacons assume the duty, not only of ruling their own congregation, but also of sharing in the government of the church universal; thus the Roman clergy tell Cyprian[94] in 250 that "we should all be on guard for the body of the whole church, whose members are scattered throughout the various provinces". Cyprian himself refers to fellow-presbyters (*conpresbyteri nostri*) as well as fellow-bishops,[95] and calls the junior clergy whether at Carthage or at Rome his brothers,[96] according to a usage which seems to have been regular since it appears also in Augustine's letters to Jerome. Before proceeding to an ordination it was Cyprian's normal practice[97] to consult his "very dear brothers", which in this case includes the laity at Carthage as well as its presbyters and deacons, somewhat as Cornelius[98] at Rome summoned his presbytery along with five visiting bishops to deal with the important matter of readmitting schismatics to church membership. This Roman presbytery was of course later to develop into the Sacred College of the cardinals of the Roman Church.

Sohm[99] was indeed convinced that every ecclesiastical council of the third century formed in principle a local congregational meeting, reinforced by the presence of leading members from other churches;[100] authority came from the local congregation, which alone had effective power to enforce decisions, but the participation of other bishops ensured that the findings would have a universal validity.

It was certainly Cyprian's ideal that clergy and people should join his episcopal colleagues in expressing the church's common mind, and this principle was put into practice whenever possible. Thus he proposed[101] to examine the martyrs' plea for absolution of the apostates with his fellow-bishops convened in council, "in accordance with the Lord's discipline, the confessors' presence and the judgment also of the people"; he told[102] his presbyters and deacons that the whole matter would be dealt with "by the bond of common counsel" when the bishops met with the clergy in the presence of the faithful people, who themselves deserved honour for their faith and godly fear; and when the African council of eighty-seven bishops met to consider the rebaptism of converted heretics, it recorded[103] that "many bishops were convened from the provinces of Africa, Numidia and Mauretania, along with presbyters and deacons, a large part of the people also being present".

But however corporate the activities of the church may be, they hinge on one essential point of reference in the bishop. When Peter,[104] on whom the church was built asked, Lord to whom shall we go?, he taught in the church's name showing,

> that although an unruly and proud multitude of the disobedient may depart, yet the church does not secede from Christ, and the church consists of people united to priest and the flock adhering to its pastor. Whence you must know that the bishop is in the church and the church in the bishop, and if a man is not with the bishop he is not in the church, and it is in vain that those beguile themselves who cheat without having the peace of God's priests and imagine that they communicate by stealth with certain persons, since the church which is one and catholic is neither rent nor divided, but is everywhere joined and unified by the glue of priests in mutual concord. Wherefore, my brother, if you consider the majesty of Christ the God who ordains priests, if you have some regard for Christ who by his will and nod and presence governs both the prelates themselves and with them the church, if you believe in the priests' innocence motivated not by human hatred but by the divine judgement, if you begin to perform even a belated penance for your rashness and pride and insolence, if you have made the fullest satisfaction to the Lord and his Christ whom I serve and to whom I offer sacrifices continually with pure and unspotted lips both under persecution and in peace, then we could consider the possibility of communicating with you while preserving our respect and fear for the divine censure, and first I would consult my Lord as to whether by his sign and prompting he will allow me to give you peace and admit you to the communion of his church.

Few prelates can ever have had such confidence either in their own inspiration or in the complete wrong-headedness of a schismatic confessor who opposed them. But the important point in this remarkable epistle is its utterly Christocentric basis.

Christ acts through his bishops, and so long as they remain in him they remain in entire harmony with one another. Cyprian expresses these ideas by saying that they hold the episcopate *in solidum*, a phrase derived from Roman jurisprudence whose exact meaning is disputed. His actual words[105] are "the episcopate is one, a part of which is held *in solidum* by each", and this is immediately followed by a sentence describing the unity of the church expanded into a multitude of cells.

Benson[106] thought that he referred to "a tenure upon a totality like that of a shareholder in some joint property", and Lacey[107] put it more briefly in terms of co-partnership or joint possession. Blakeney[108] interpreted the phrase to mean "as a corporation", commenting that "when two parties have borrowed and guaranteed the same sum of money, both are responsible *in solidum* (for the whole), the whole obligation rests on both as in an unlimited company". Koch[109] expressed himself more vaguely, saying that each bishop shares the one episcopal office in so far as he is in communion with the episcopate as a whole, but Casel[110] insisted that the phrase is a legal one, referring to a right or duty of several persons which each has in entirety, and he offered the interpretation that, since all bishops share the episcopate in such a way that each has the whole it follows that there can only be one bishop in one place. Bardy[111] agreed on the words' juridical value, but saw the joint participation of every bishop in all the episcopal powers as a pointer to the importance of councils for Cyprian's ecclesiology.

Le Moyne[112] was against an interpretation that rested too strictly on the language of Roman law, and maintained that the phrase did not refer to the impossibility of having two bishops in a single place; instead he preferred to connect it with the personal unity of bishops among themselves and so with the unique episcopal office.

Greenslade,[113] while admitting the phrase's legal origin, held that Cyprian did not use it with a lawyer's precision, and hence it is difficult to translate; in the sense of solidary obligation it means that each bishop must act with responsibility to the whole college, but in terms of tenure upon a totality the meaning is that every bishop has his episcopate entire; and *episcopatus* can refer both to the episcopal college, of which Cyprian would chiefly think in the year 251, and to the powers of an individual bishop, which would be uppermost in his mind in 256.

But Bévenot[114] has returned to the full emphasis on juristic phraseology. He refers to the *Digest* as preserving citations from the great lawyers of the period, and insists that, while liability *in solidum* can apply to several persons, ownership *in solidum* can belong only to one. Thus Ulpian[115] states that joint creditors or debtors may each be entitled or liable *in solidum* or they may be so only for a fraction. (Le Moyne[116] had previously doubted whether this citation is relevant, since it envisages the obligation of a person whereas Cyprian was describing the possession of a thing; but to this it may be replied that a thing, namely the episcopate, is the object of the personal obligation here involved.) Ulpian further states[117] that things can only be possessed *in solidum* if owned by a single person, while a joint-owner does not hold in this particular way even if he has certain rights over the whole property. (Le Moyne commented that the reference here is to ownership as opposed to use, and he added that both of these citations consider a whole object whereas Cyprian is speaking of a part; but here the answer must surely be that the part of the episcopate held by each bishop is in fact the whole, since even when it is used or exercised locally, it like the church remains at all times one and indivisible.) Another citation[118] from Roman law states that a paterfamilias may be liable *in solidum* or only in part for the conduct of his son or slave; and Paulus[119] states that if a slave is jointly owned by several masters, the property which he may earn belongs *in solidum* to the one as whose agent he was acting.

It seems that Cyprian, having said that the episcopate is a unity, goes on to say that each local manifestation of it is wielded indivisibly by the local bishop. Bévenot[120] insists, in opposition to Greenslade, that *episcopatus* in Cyprian's writings never means "the body of bishops", but only the episcopal power which is exercised throughout the church universal, its parts being those exercised by each individual bishop in his own congregation. It is therefore held by each "in totality", in such a way that no rival bishop can be established in any see; the part is in fact always the whole. When he wrote his *De unitate*, Cyprian thought of a local situation, at Carthage or at Rome, and he sought to prove that schism there would have a universal impact.

Mascall has recently[121] remarked that Cyprian's language implies a concept of the episcopate as a living organism. But if so, it has a deeper meaning than Mascall apparently envisages: more than joint occupancy of the one Petrine position by each episcopal incumbent of Peter's chair, and more than the relation subsisting between a bishop and his colleagues or between all bishops and the church. It signifies in essence that the episcopate is Christ's territorial embodiment, so that the one episcopate is his alone; and if a man is to be regarded as a bishop, he must first of all be found in Christ.

IV

THE CHURCH AND THE CHURCHES

CYPRIAN DOES NOT often apply the epithet *sancta* (holy) to the church. At first sight this may seem surprising, but the reason is actually plain: the holiness of the church and of its bishops is so much a presupposition of his whole ecclesiology that he takes it for granted without the need for frequent or specific mention. On several occasions[1] he calls the church the house of God or of faith (*domus Dei*, *domus fidei*); it is the womb, root, origin or head (*matrix, radix, origo, caput*); from another aspect it is the spouse of Christ (*sponsa Christi*)[2] so that heresy or schism is tantamount to adultery.[3] Built and founded upon Peter, the *ecclesia una*, whether it refers to the church universal or to a local congregation,[4] is unique.

But his most frequent and best-loved concept is that of the church as mother. From his epistles alone[5] the following instances may be cited: mother church glories in the confessors' faith and courage, she sheds tears for the ruin and fall of many, the mother must first receive peace from God before she considers the confessors' appeal for leniency to the lapsed, loyal clergy remain with mother church and receive stipends from her bishop, the enemies of mother church blaspheme against the heavenly Father, and before a man can have God as his Father he must have the church as mother. The glorious fertility of mother church is increased, in Cyprian's view,[6] when many virgins are added to her membership. Elsewhere[7] apostate parents who take their Christian children to pagan sacrifices are said to deny on the child's behalf both mother church and God the Father. And the clearest parallel between the Fatherhood of God and the church's motherhood is expressed in the treatise on church unity:[8]

The spouse of Christ cannot become an adulteress, for she is undefiled and chaste. She has only known one house and preserves with modest chastity the holiness of a single room. It is she who keeps us for God and enrols in his kingdom the children whom she bore. Whoever separates from the church in joining an adulteress is beyond the scope of promises granted to the church, and if he leaves the church of Christ he will not attain to Christ's rewards. He is a foreigner, an outsider and a foe. He who does not have the church as his mother cannot have God as Father.

For scriptural proof of this famous phrase, Cyprian refers to the necessity of being within Noah's ark[9] in order to escape the deluge, and he quotes Christ's words in Matt. 12: 30, "Whoever is not with me is against me, and he who does not gather with me scatters." But his fundamental proof occurs a sentence later, when he cites John 10: 30, "I and the Father are one"; the church's unity is based on that of God.

The motherhood of the church, no less than her unity, is associated with the person of the bishop, for he is the normal minister of baptism in which her children are spiritually born. When Cornelius was faced by a rival bishop at Rome, Cyprian[10] gave instruction to travellers so that they would be able to "recognize and adhere to the womb and root of the church catholic"; and he proceeded to explain himself in less florid language by saying that as soon as he had verified the validity of the election, he advised his colleagues to maintain the church's unity by holding communion with Cornelius. Peter disclosed[11] this "sacrament of unity"[12] when he drew a comparison between salvation in baptism and salvation in Noah's ark; it is symbolized in the gospel by Christ's robe which could not be torn apart, and it provides an image on earth of the celestial mystery[13] of the Triune Godhead. In matters both divine and human it signifies uniqueness, a word for which the French[14] have a more euphonious equivalent in *unicité*; from this feature catholicity is derived, both local and universal, since there is "one God and one Christ and one church and one *cathedra*",[15] "one baptism, one Holy Spirit and (again) one Church, founded with the source and structure of unity by our Lord Christ on Peter".[16] This must not be taken to imply a papal supremacy, for here "the one church is in the first instance the particular or local church";[17] but the local church is catholic because it is not independent, forming a cell of "the one church divided into many members throughout the entire world".[18]

Harnack[19] scarcely did justice to Cyprian's ecclesiology when he described it as "an imitation of the conception of a political empire, *viz.* one great aristocratically governed state with an ideal head", and went on to suggest that "the limitation of the church to the community ruled by bishops was the result of the Novatian crisis".

It was much more mystical than political, and Cyprian himself would have denied that it resulted from passing circumstances, since he was careful to derive it from the sources of scripture and tradition.

"For it is our tradition," he writes,[20] "that there is one God, one Christ, one hope, one faith, one church and one baptism ministered only in the one church, and if a man departs from this he must needs be found with heretics, in supporting whom against the church he assails the sacrament of divine tradition. We see the sacrament of this unity expressed even by the Song of Songs (4: 12–13) in the person of Christ who says, A garden enclosed is my sister, my spouse, a fountain sealed, a well of living water, a paradise with the fruit of apples . . . in the same way Peter himself also demonstrating and vindicating the unity . . . says (1 Pet. 3, 20–21), In the ark of Noah few, that is eight souls of men, were saved by water, and likewise you also are saved by baptism. . . ."

This quotation alone is enough to refute Jalland's view[21] that "with Cyprian the content of the original *paradosis* has almost wholly lost its former doctrinal character, and has instead become a *paradosis* of unity, i.e. of discipline". The unity is indeed enforced by discipline, but it is based on doctrine and ultimately on the doctrine of monotheism; it is drawn from scripture, whose teaching is regarded by Cyprian as the Christian law. Quoting Joshua 1: 8 ("This book of the law shall not depart out of your mouth"), he defines[22] tradition as "descending from the authority of the Lord and of the gospel, and coming from the apostles' mandates and epistles". In other words, he virtually identifies tradition with scripture.

The method of compiling proof-texts, which he had early employed in his *Testimonia*, is repeated in the long address to Fortunatus, *De exhortatione martyrii*, which he describes[23] as "not so much a treatise as the material for making one . . . the very wool and purple from the Lamb by whom we are redeemed and made alive". In expounding the church's unity his material is always drawn from scripture, favourite texts being these:[24] Song 6: 9 ("my dove is one . . .") and 4: 12 ("A garden enclosed is my sister . . ."), 1 Pet. 3: 20–21 (the ark of Noah), and Eph. 5: 25–26 ("Christ loved the church and gave himself for it, that he might sanctify and cleanse it with the laver of water"). Behind both scripture and tradition he hears the voice of Christ; "This is my beloved Son," he quotes[25] from Matt. 17: 5 and continues,

Wherefore if Christ alone is to be heard, we should not pay attention to what another before us may have thought fit to do, but to what Christ who is before all first did.

In line with this Christocentric attitude, Cyprian finds[26] a figure of church unity in the allegorical exegesis of Christ's seamless robe, so different from the rent garments of Israel's tribes, and traces[27] sacra-

mental symbols of the same in the many grains which make one
bread, or the many grapes pressed into one cup. But if the church is
united as one body in a single Lord, the articulation of its many
members is not ossified into a leaden uniformity. "While the bond of
concord lasts and the undivided sacrament of the catholic church abides,
each bishop controls and directs his own activity as one who will give
an account of his purpose to the Lord."[28]

If there is one God and Christ and in consequence one church, there
is also one episcopal chair, one altar and one priesthood,[29] and this is a
concept which implies not only the unanimity but also the independence of the bishops. On the one hand, there is a distinct flock with its
one pastor in each place; on the other, the flesh of Christ cannot be
divided, but is universally eaten like the paschal lamb in a single
house.[30] The people are joined into a solid unity of the body[31] by the
glue of concord, and this unity cannot be broken nor can the one body
be divided, because a member separated from the *matrix* cannot live
apart. All therefore have an earnest duty[32] to join in obeying the pre-
cepts of their common Lord.

Only within this sphere of the divine covenant can the divine promises be fulfilled, and thus the church as Christ's body is the exclusive
vehicle of grace. Outside it there is no valid baptism[33] since holy church
is the sole abode of the Holy Spirit, who cannot be bestowed by those
in whom he does not dwell; the pretended ministry of unclean hands
does not sanctify, but the "one baptism" of scripture is restricted to the
one church of Christ. Cyprian quotes[34] from the baptismal creed in the
form currently used by Christians of North Africa, "Dost thou believe
in eternal life and remission of sins through holy church?" as proof
that it is only within the church that sins can be forgiven. And yet
absolution, by imposition of hands after confession and performance of
the penance due, must be obtained[35] before communicating, if the
penitent is not to incur the extreme peril of an unworthy communion. "The sinner's satisfactions had efficacy only when completed
by the absolution of the bishop,"[36] and episcopal action even when
irregular is always valid,[37] whereas presbyters cannot absolve unless
they have their own bishop's authority.

It is natural that Cyprian should lay more emphasis than Tertullian
does on the judicial aspect of absolution; but ultimately the church
secures a sinner's pardon solely through her offering of prayers, among
which those of the martyrs[38] are particularly potent. In the meanwhile
the actions of the clergy are provisional, without prejudging any deci-

sion of the Lord who is to come again, and who is never deceived although men may be cheated by a feigned repentance.[39] For serious sins, grievous penance is essential in view of the last judgement,[40] but Cyprian never pretends that a human verdict is final, and however necessary sacerdotal absolution may be, this must not usurp the prerogative of Christ. Indeed in his earlier days[41] Cyprian had maintained that sins committed against God cannot be remitted in the church; it was only when faced by the problem of dealing with a multitude of lapsed Christians that he came to mitigate the strict Novatianist position.

None the less he continued to insist[42] that God as the sole Redeemer alone has the prerogative of mercy; he is pleased to dispense it through the instrumentality of his ministers; but outside the church there is no salvation.[43] Nor is there any Christianity beyond the confines of the church, and Cyprian writes,[44] "You must know in the first place that we should not be curious about what Novatian teaches, since he teaches outside—whoever he is and whatever his character may be, he is not a Christian if he is not in Christ's church." The whole secular world and all the sects are devoid of sanctifying grace:

> Although there can be no other than the one baptism, they (the schismatics) imagine that they can baptize; after deserting the fountain of life, they promise the grace of living and saving water. Men are not washed there but rather defiled, nor are sins purged but only increased; that nativity does not bear children for God but for the devil.[45]

This note of rigid severity, which rings through Cyprian's doctrine of the church, echoes the anguish of a loving heart at the perverse divisions caused by human sin. He compares[46] schismatic presbyters, who corrupt the church's chastity with adulterous teaching, to those Jewish elders who assailed the virtue of Susannah. He says that ordination performed outside the church is illicit;[47] and since God does not hear sinners (John 9: 31), a bishop who falls into mortal sin loses his episcopate[48] and must by every means be excluded[49] from the altar and from contact with the brethren. He says[50] that confessors if guilty of schism cannot reach the reward of glory, and even martyrdom if suffered outside the church obtains no crown.

> The apostate sinned once but he (the schismatic) sins daily. And if an apostate turns into a martyr he can obtain the promise of the kingdom, but a schismatic, if he is executed outside the church, cannot attain to the church's rewards.[51]

For though he gives his body to be burned, and has not the charity which is inseparable from unity, it profits him nothing.

> The grave and inexpiable guilt of discord is not purged by passion . . . and he who has not charity does not have God.[52]

From this it follows that disunity is the gravest sin which it is possible for Christians to commit.

> He who breaks Christ's peace and concord acts against Christ, and Christ's church is scattered by him who gathers elsewhere beyond its pale. The Lord says, I and the Father are one (John 10: 30). . . . And does anyone believe that this unity, descending from the divine consistency and co-inhering with celestial mysteries, can be divided in the church and separated by the clash of contending wills? He who does not preserve this unity, preserves neither God's law, nor faith in the Father and the Son, nor life itself and salvation.[53]

The guilt of schism is not mitigated even if the schismatic retains orthodox doctrine.[54] And it is virtually impossible for him to do so, since in justifying his position he is obliged to expound texts of scripture in isolation from their context;[55] Matt. 18: 20 must be read in the light of the preceding verse, which shows that the gathering of two or three in Christ's name does not refer to any separate conventicle, but to the unanimity which must in all places characterize a Christian group.

> And how can two or three gather in the name of Christ, when it is obvious that they have separated from Christ and from his gospel? For we did not secede from them but they from us, and since heresies and schisms are of recent birth, they have left the head and source of truth when they set up their diversity of conventicles. But the Lord speaks about his church and to those that are within it. . . . He only promised his presence with two or three if they are simple-hearted and peaceful, fearing God and keeping his commandments.[56]

Schismatics suffer the punishment of Korah, Dathan and Abiram,[57] who tried to sacrifice in opposition to Moses and Aaron the priest. And it is of no avail for those outside the church to pretend that they know the Trinity whom the church confesses:

> For Korah, Dathan and Abiram knew the same God as did Aaron the priest and Moses, living under an identical law and religion . . . but since, in transgressing the ministry proper to their station, they claimed authority to sacrifice in competition with Aaron the priest, who had received a legitimate priesthood by the approval of God and ordination of the Lord, they were divinely smitten and at once . . . suffered the penalty.[58]

53

It is because of sin that the bread and cup of Christ, with all his grace, have been transferred from the Jewish people to the Christian church.[59] Heresy and schism are inventions of the devil, who can transform himself into an angel of light, but will be recognized in his true colours by those that return to the source of truth, and seek the head, and preserve the teaching of the heavenly Master.[60] Just as Cain's offering was rejected, so a man who does not live in peace with his brethren will not find peace with God.[61] Such a man is self-condemned and must be shunned,

> whoever he may be, if separated from the church; he is perverse and sinful and damned by his own action, unless one imagines that he can be with Christ when he opposes Christ's priests and secedes both from his clergy and from the fellowship of his flock.[62]

Schisms are caused by evil character, perverse thoughts and perfidy, which God permits to bear their divisive fruits because he will not interfere with human freedom.

> Let no one imagine that good men can depart out of the church; wind does not blow away the wheat . . . (10). The reason why heresies have often happened and are still with us is that a perverse mind knows no peace and divisive treason does not maintain unity. God allows and suffers this to occur while private judgement remains free. . . . These are the people who set themselves up among rash associates without divine order, who establish themselves as prelates with no rule of ordination and who, when no one bestows the episcopate, assume to themselves the name of bishop.[63]

More precisely, the cause of schism is disobedience to the clergy in choosing a rival bishop against divine law.

> Heresies have arisen and schisms been produced from no other source than disobedience to the priest of God, when men cease to think of one priest at a time and one judge as Christ's vicar in the church; but if the whole brotherhood obeyed him in accordance with divine teaching, no one would take any step against the college of priests, no one after God's verdict, the people's assent and the agreement of episcopal colleagues, would make himself judge not of the bishops but of God, no one would rend Christ's church by breaking unity, no one in proud self-will would found a new heresy by himself outside; unless anyone is so rash in sacrilege and corrupt in mind as to think that a priest can be made without God's verdict, when the Lord says in the gospel that . . . not one sparrow falls to the ground without the Father's will (Matt. 10: 29).[64]

Self-will coupled with disdain for prelates is the source of schismatic behaviour, leading to the profanity of a rival altar and rebellion against unity and peace.[65] Such according to Cyprian is the psychology of schism, the pathological aspect of ecclesiastical man. And Benson[66] rightly adds that lapsed or schismatic clergy, who could only be re-admitted to the church as laymen,[67] would be particularly prone to seek further clerical employment "in some aggressive sect". Other reasons for separation might stem from a presbyter's resentment at what he regarded as episcopal arrogance.[68] Novatus supported the lax party at Carthage and the rigorists at Rome very possibly because he was con-cerned, not with discipline of the lapsed in either city, but with main-taining the power of presbyters independently of their bishop; in Car-thage he got Felicissimus as his deacon,[69] and in Rome he arranged for consecration of the schismatic Novatian by three rural bishops who, Cornelius says,[70] were drunk. The utter falsity of Novatian's position is thus described by Cyprian:[71]

> ... unless you consider as bishop a man who strove through ambition to be made an adulterous and foreign bishop by the hands of runaways, when there was already a bishop in the church consecrated by sixteen colleagues, and although one church with many cells descends from Christ throughout the whole world, together with one episcopate shared by the harmonious multitude of many bishops, this man ... tries to found a human church ... and sends out his new apostles ... daring to create other pseudo-bishops in place of (the legitimate incumbents). ... But he could not keep his bishopric, even supposing he had formerly been consecrated by the body of his col-leagues, if he departs from church unity. ... Thus ... the man who separates himself from the bond of the church and the college of priests can have neither the authority nor the honour of a bishop, because he did not mean to preserve the unity and peace of the episcopate.

Those who wish to perish in schism must perish by themselves alone, cut off from the church which they have forsaken, and devoid of bishops against whose office they rebel.[72] Far different is the "great mystery" of Christ who forms one flesh with the church his bride.[73]

It was this passionate plea for unity in love which enabled Augus-tine[74] to turn the tables on the Donatists' appeal to Cyprian. They had supported their position with his insistence on the church's holiness, although the personal record of several of their leaders made such sup-port a mockery, but Augustine refuted them by quoting Cyprian's ab-horrence of enmity and schism. "The authority of Cyprian does not frighten me", he writes, "because I am refreshed by his humility." St. Peter refused to contend with St. Paul, even if the former apostle tried to break what was later to become the church's rule when he asked Gentiles to practise Jewish customs; and Cyprian was a lesser man doing a lesser thing when he broke a rule, later to be adopted by the whole church, and compelled heretics or schismatics to be baptized afresh. "Do not then cast Cyprian's authority in our teeth when you demand rebaptism, but join us in following Cyprian's example for the preservation of unity."

The Bishop of Carthage had maintained that outside the church there could be no "just and lawful baptism"; Augustine agrees, but contends that the sects do have a baptism which is "unjust and illicit". Cyprian's mistake was that he did not distinguish the sacrament itself from its effect or use; the catholic church has now corrected what was a relatively minor error, but his teaching of charity stands firm. In his *Retractions*[75] Augustine adds that the church's holiness will only be made perfect in a state of glory, but that at present she is a mixed society of good and evil members. Here, however, he did no more than quote Cyprian, who had already[76] applied to the state of the church militant both the parable of the wheat and tares and the description in 2 Tim. 2: 20 of the vessels unto honour or dishonour; "Cyprian's was the first exposition of these passages of scripture as presenting the type of the conditions of church society,"[77] so that in this cardinal point of his anti-Donatist polemic Augustine merely followed his predecessor's lead.

Cyprian did not create a new doctrine of the church in order to solve his own agonizing problems, but he illumined old doctrines with "that sense of love and feeling after unity which seemed to Augustine the most special characteristic of the man".[78] If he had an evangelical fervour of the spirit and a puritan desire for holiness, he also firmly believed in the principles of catholicity.

Now the earliest recorded use of the phrase "catholic church" occurs in the letters of Ignatius,[79] where it refers to the church universal as opposed to a local congregation, and the essential mark of catholicity is the presence of Jesus Christ. But by the third century[80] the bishop had become its essential feature, and "catholic church" could mean a local gathering of orthodox believers. Ignatius stands near the beginning of a process by which the institutional aspect of episcopacy was made more prominent; in his day heresy was still incipient and the boundaries of Christendom were less rigidly defined. Cyprian lived in an age of sectarianism, and although it would be quite wrong to imagine that he regarded the catholic church as one denomination among many, it is none the less clear that he had to face a painful situation in which the one true church no longer embraced all who professed the Christian name.

He dealt with the problem of schism by equating it with heresy, and denied the title of Christian to any who separated from his church. He could do so because of his complete conviction that Christ was present with him and not with his opponents. Hence he experienced an exultant joy on hearing[81] that two schismatic confessors had returned to the church catholic, abandoning their temporary association with "betrayers of the faith and assailants of the church", and showing by their return that the *ecclesia catholica* is one and indivisible.

Most often he wrote and thought in terms of the local congregation, but he never allowed it to restrict his wider vision[82] of the universal church; because this was founded upon Peter it is one, and because it is one, unity must subsist both within and between its territorial cells. There is one episcopate shared by many bishops but only one bishop in each place, and there is one church embodied in many congregations whose multiplicity presupposes unity.[83] This unity is not produced by federating autonomous individuals. On the contrary, just as Peter was prior to the episcopate, so "the universal church is logically prior to the local churches and to individual Christians".[84]

It must again be emphasized that, when Cyprian speaks of the primacy or the chair of Peter, he does not employ these terms in the sense which they would normally bear today. Peter's primacy is no more than a temporal priority before all other believers, and his one chair is found in every orthodox see.

Again, the bishop whom Cyprian envisages is totally unlike a modern diocesan; he is the pastor of a parish, assisted by a session of ruling elders and advised by regular meetings of his congregation. But to call him a pastor may create the wrong impression, and it would be better to follow Cyprian's own usage in describing the bishop as a priest, provided one remembers that this sacerdotalism in the liturgy does not imply a clerical domination in church government. For Sohm[85] has produced adequate evidence to substantiate his thesis that church councils in the third century were always congregational meetings, enlarged and universalized by the presence of bishops from other churches. This became particularly obvious at episcopal elections, when neighbouring bishops assisted the local clergy and people to choose a candidate, and then laid hands upon him to set the seal of their approval.

But a similar type of gathering was used for all church purposes, a good example being provided[86] by the plenary council of eighty-seven African bishops, whose decision to baptize converted heretics was taken "along with presbyters and deacons and a large part also of the people". This method of procedure was inevitable, since the local congregation formed the only effective instrument of discipline, but in order to maintain unity other churches participated in the congregational meeting through their bishops.

Cyprian regarded the ideal purpose of councils as "a gathering into one (*in unum convenire*)",[87] or in Küng's[88] phrase as expressing the "totality of the consciousness of the church", and he himself was so "loyal to the deliberative power he had evoked"[89] that he sometimes abandoned his own suggestions and bowed to a conciliar verdict with which he had at first disagreed. He would certainly have applauded a description of the second Vatican Council by Pope John XXIII as "the great reunion of the Christian people",[90] because it is when the people gathers into one that the church's unity is clearly seen.

From such considerations the Abbot of Downside[91] deduced that Cyprian implicitly taught the infallibility of the church; outside it there is no salvation, but it excludes from membership those who dissent from its doctrine, and therefore God who wills salvation must be expected to ensure that its doctrines are always sound. Cyprian never expresses himself in such language, and it is doubtful whether he would have accepted the argument as a logical deduction from his views.

Any congregational meeting might on his theory fall into doctrinal error, and so long as men possess freewill the entire episcopate could simultaneously become heretical. The possibility is indeed remote, but it is not logically excluded. And yet the individual believer has a duty to separate from his bishop if the latter falls from grace, and should the Christian decide to do so he has no ultimate guidance other than his own private judgement. This is the direct personal responsibility which laymen, no less than bishops, owe to God.

It is a perilous decision, for if taken wrongly it leads to the mortal sin of schism. But it is not in fact ever to be made in isolation, since a norm is provided by the teaching of scripture and the tradition of the church, as expressing the voice of Christ interpreted through the common mind of all the brethren. Indeed the isolated Christian, unless he should turn out to be an *Athanasius contra mundum*, is a contradiction in terms, and the church remains prior to the individual. Prophecies may fail and tongues may cease and knowledge may vanish away; but charity abides, and he who dwells in love continues in God.

But critics have complained that Cyprian's theory of the church is unworkable in practice. Bévenot[92] remarks that he had been elevated too quickly to a bishopric, while he still lacked "that long experience of life in the church" which could have made him more worldly wise. The same author[93] warns against the danger of constructing out of particular phrases a system of "Cyprian's thought"; he was not a systematic theologian and his ardent ideas are on occasion inconsistent. Batiffol[94] argues that if Cyprian had logically followed out the decision which his council reached in the case of the Spanish appeal,[95] he would have told the congregation at Arles to separate from their schismatic bishop Marcian, and would then have written to the bishops of the province advising them to consecrate a successor; instead he wrote to Pope Stephen,[96] which suggests that the appeal to Rome had been a regular practice and that Cyprian broke this normal rule by innovating in the Spanish case.

Now it is certainly true that Cyprian's conduct differed on different occasions, but he was probably obliged to change his tactics because of the personal circumstances involved. He believed that unity would continue so long as all Christians obeyed the law of God, listened to the voice of Christ, and lived in the Holy Spirit, and this belief is obviously true; however, it may well be objected that such ideals are unpractical for a church of ordinary mortals and would work only in a society of saints.

"As councils have no compelling force, as the Pope need not be obeyed unless one happens to agree with him", writes Chapman,[97] "there is no remedy left for disorder. Yet Cyprian has complete confidence in the divine ordination of church unity, and in the moral unanimity of bishops 'glued together'. I fear it was the shortness of his experience which made it possible to put forward a theory which no one has ever held before or since. This is why I think 'St. Cyprian's theory of the episcopate' is of no importance except for his own biography."

This comment is historically unjust. Cyprian was earnestly quoted as an authority by both catholics and protestants at the time of the Reformation, and if his ecclesiology has proved so many-sided, this may indicate that it has an ecumenical significance today.

It is certainly true[98] that his theology is unsystematic and often implied rather than expressed in full. But his stature as a churchman appears from the fact that he was the only important Latin author among the Christians of his century who did not fall into a state of heresy or schism. He was mature and well-educated by the time of his conversion, and his *Testimonia* already employ the clear-cut method of citing proof-texts from the Bible. If he was too immersed in practical affairs to have an opportunity, during his short episcopate, of developing into a really great theologican, his thinking does have a luminous centre in the one visible church as essential to salvation. Indeed it may be argued that his doctrine of the church is more consistent than that of Augustine, whatever problems it may have to face in practice.

> "It is strictly logical", argues Willis,[99] "to hold that only within the fold of Christ can the sheep be fed; and the Cyprianic scheme avoids all the difficulties of application inherent in the more subtle doctrine of Saint Augustine. Strong in theory, however, it was quite likely in practice . . . to lead to schism through disagreement between groups of bishops."

But one has only to consider the later schism between East and West to realize that, even on more "subtle" theories, division can result when groups of bishops disagree. What became the catholic doctrine raises acute problems about the coherence of church, ministry and sacraments, and "there is much to be said for Cyprian's attempt to hold these elements together, though we may be driven to a different conception of the church if we are to do so"[100] in the modern world.

Augustine's critique of the Cyprianic theology of baptism[101] is suggestive of a wider application. When Cyprian insisted that baptism must be either ecclesiastical or null, he saw the problem in terms of too rigid a separation into white or black; and when Augustine allowed that schismatic baptism might be valid although inefficacious, he painted a more human picture in varying shades of grey. Applied to ecclesiology, the Augustinian approach might suggest that there is no absolute distinction between church and sect, but that all possess the church's attributes and graces to a greater or a less degree.

But it must always be remembered that Cyprian combined catholic churchmanship with prophetic vision, and despite his institutional language, he thought of an ideal church, a church of the Spirit, whom the institution upon earth embodies.[102] And for him the solution is to be found in terms not of theology but of love: *qui caritatem non habet, Deum non habet.*[103]

V

THE APPEAL TO CYPRIAN AT THE REFORMATION

The Church of the first three centuries, like that of the New Testament, contained elements which could be variously described as episcopal, presbyterian or congregationalist. Its theology was enriched by the juxtaposition of Greek and Latin, the former more mystical and laying stress upon the Incarnation, the latter more legalistic and placing its central emphasis upon the Cross. Even after the Greek East had separated from the Latin West, medieval Christendom in Western Europe retained trends that were liberal or evangelical as well as catholic. And if these different tendencies largely separated at the Reformation, there was still much common ground between an evangelical catholic like Contarini and a liberal protestant like Melanchthon. Indeed, as the Reformed Churches settled down into established institutions they displayed many features of catholicism; and the Roman communion, having reformed itself at Trent, reacquired much of the puritan discipline which had characterized the ancient church. It is therefore not surprising that all parties should have appealed, not only to the Fathers in general, but in particular to the many-sided churchmanship of Cyprian. Augustine, so evangelical and at the same time so catholic, provided a mine of polemical ammunition; but Cyprian had anticipated him at many points, and he also was an authority whom everyone might desire to quote.

Church historians of the sixteenth century are on the whole disappointing in their account of Cyprian. From the Lutheran side, the Magdeburg Centuries give[1] a straightforward account of his life as "a most diligent . . . and faithful guardian of his church", followed by a list of writings some of which are spurious; they outline his doctrine, noting with approval that "he had the right opinion of the presence of Christ's true Body and Blood in the Supper", and remarking that when he taught church unity, he defined the church as "an assembly of believers in Christ who are joined and united through this faith"; they criticize a few faults, such as his use of Tertullian's language in calling penances "satisfactions", his assertion of freewill and his excessive stress

E   61

on good works; and after summarizing his controversies, in particular that with Pope Stephen on rebaptism, they praise his fervent oratory and glorious martyrdom. Earlier, in a passage[2] describing third-century doctrine, they misrepresent his attitude to Rome:

> Elsewhere he expressly says, and that without any foundation of Holy Scripture, that the Roman church should be recognized by all others as the womb and root of the church catholic. Moreover he calls it the principal church, the chair of Peter, from which the sacerdotal unity arose. However in the same place he denies that cases should be taken on appeal to Rome for judgement. But elsewhere he repeatedly remarks that the church was founded upon Peter.

A chapter[3] dealing with the consociation of churches quotes Cyprian almost in every paragraph, and thirty-nine times in all, with reference to unity at the local, provincial and ecumenical levels; he is depicted as admonishing other bishops of their duty, and accusing Stephen of contumacy and presumption when he defended an unrighteous custom; his rejection of a papal primacy is proved from the facts that he called Cornelius his brother, reproved the Roman bishop, and asserted the independent authority of the Africans in discipline; and his teaching on episcopal equality is illustrated from the friendly argument between St. Peter and St. Paul. If he regarded Rome as the principal church and Peter's chair, he did not mean to imply that Rome possesses a divine jurisdiction or primacy, and she is the church's womb and root in the sense that she is best situated to preserve unity and love. The very different tone of this interpretation from that in the passage previously cited suggests that it was written by a different member of the Magdeburg team.

The learned Roman Catholic historian Baronius[4] points out that very soon after his conversion, Cyprian showed a profound knowledge of scripture and theology, and unless this was due to a miracle he must have studied the Bible while he was still a pagan; he was also addicted to the study of Tertullian, but selected wisely from that writer, "purging his doctrine in the furnace of the Holy Spirit in order to separate gold from mud".[5] During the papal vacancy of 253, letters from the Roman clergy showed a pastoral concern for the North African churches,[6] and Cyprian consulted Rome "as one who desired to have everything approved by the judgement of the Roman church . . . and sought to silence objectors by relying on the authority of the primatial see";[7] decrees of the Roman synod were accepted by all the churches because "all understood so much authority to reside in the See of Peter that the entire catholic world, though spread both far and wide, undoubtedly considered that it must observe whatever decision it knew to flow from Peter's chair".[8] Cornelius was modest in not desiring the Roman bishopric at a time when Decius had said that he would rather face a rival Emperor than the Pope, and this modesty showed him to be divinely chosen for the office; he was also consecrated at the hands of many bishops, by the judgement of God and Christ, with the testimony of almost all the clergy and the suffrage of the people then present, when the place of Peter was vacant, and his title was therefore so obviously valid that any rival Pope must be an intruder.[9] Cyprian wrote his *De unitate* as a great "wedge and tower" against the onslaught of sectarians; it was designed to deal not only with the opposition of Novatian, but also with all schisms, "by showing that there can only be one church, which must be recognized in Peter's chair, with the remainder joined to it as members to their head"; anyone not in communion with the chair of Peter is a heretic, and "after many arguments drawn from Holy Scripture, (Cyprian) adds that the primacy was given to Peter. . . ."[10] The appeal of the Spanish bishops to Rome illustrates the papal jurisdiction, which Cyprian did not deny although he argued that Pope Stephen was ignorant of the true facts behind this case.[11] When dealing with Marcian of Arles, Cyprian wrote to Stephen "because he knew that to depose a metropolitan required the jurisdiction of the Roman Pontiff as prince of all the bishops".[12] And the baptismal controversy "clearly evidenced the weight of authority residing in Peter's successor"[13] because here Stephen successfully withstood widespread criticism from both East and West; Cyprian and his synod must have assumed that the question of rebaptism was not *de fide*, since otherwise in opposing Rome they would have been claiming the right to make themselves heretics;[14] they did not regard the Roman practice on baptism as apostolic, but even so it must have been an attack of ill-temper which impelled Cyprian, that saint who always sought the preservation of charity, to take the step he took.[15]

If church historians gave comparatively little space to Cyprian, he soon occupied the attention of divines. As early as the Leipzig Disputation of 1519, Luther cited seven of Cyprian's letters[16] to prove that he always called Cornelius "brother" and not "lord", that no bishop should exercise a tyranny over others, and that Peter had nothing more than a precedence of honour. Sample passages are conveniently translated into English by Hillerbrand:[17]

5th July 1519, 2 o'clock in the afternoon.

Luther . . . A word also about this proposition, "It is not necessary for salvation to believe that the Roman Church is superior to others." As far as I am concerned, it makes no difference whether this has been held by Wiclif or Huss. I know that Gregory of Nazianzus, Basil of Caesarea, Epiphanius, Cyprian and numerous other Greek bishops are among the redeemed, even though they did not believe this article. . . .

6th July, 7 o'clock in the morning.

Eck . . . I said earlier that Peter was by divine law the prince of the apostles according to Matth. 16, and cited Jerome, Bernard, Leo and Cyprian, concerning whom (Luther) did not respond. None the less he himself writes in his booklet that St. Cyprian was of the opinion that the church was founded upon the rock; he dared to add that St. Cyprian was here in error. . . . Cyprian clearly calls, in his 8th letter to Cornelius (i.e. *Ep.* 48, 3) the Roman Church the mother and root of the others. . . .

On a later occasion[18] Luther proved that church councils are not infallible, because the African council under Cyprian erred on the question of rebaptism, and in his so-called *Bull of Reformation* (1522)[19] he argued that Irenaeus, Cyprian, Ambrose and Augustine were pastors of a single city, not feudal lords like prelates of the Roman obedience. Cyprian is not an author frequently cited by Luther. But as a specimen of his use in exegesis, it may be noted that there are four Cyprianic references in the commentary on the last seven chapters of Genesis: two on the lurid topic of martyrdom and dreams, one on *subintroductae* or "spiritual brides", and one on Cyprian's offensive employment of the term "satisfactions". More characteristic is a quotation from the *De mortalitate*[20] in lectures on the Epistle to the Hebrews given in 1517–18,[21] which Luther uses to show the strength and victory of faith in face of death, judgement and the fear of hell; but the soul "should rather desire and even hope for the speeding hand of death to hasten its journey to Christ", and the Reformer comments "this is what Cyprian says—the consolation of death". In his *Explanation of the Ninety-five Theses* Luther refers to Cyprian four times on the subject of church discipline. And near the start of the *Babylonian Captivity*[22] he quotes the *De lapsis* in favour of communion in both kinds. In the Lutheran *Large Catechism* (Part II, art. iii, para. 42) the church is described as "the mother that begets and bears every Christian"; and the third article of the *Augsburg Confession* uses language reminiscent of Cyprian[23] when it calls Christ the *hostia* or Host.

Anabaptists and other radicals were less anxious than Lutherans to cite the authority of Cyprian. In a letter to John Campanus (1531) Sebastian Franck[24] complained that the wolves whom Paul prophesied would fall upon Christ's flock are "highly famous doctors" such as Clement, Irenaeus, Tertullian, Cyprian, Chrysostom, Hilary, Cyril and Origen, whose writings are "utterly filled with commandments, laws, sacramental elements and all kinds of human inventions". There was however one point on which Anabaptists naturally appealed to Cyprian, and this was his teaching that converts ought to be re-baptized. Bucer conceded that the saint had been an Anabaptist him-self, but as the Fathers were not infallible this sad error could be granted.[25] Those radicals who studied Cyprian carefully soon found that he had approved the baptism of infants, which of course conflicted with their own position; but Hübmaier "faultily cites . . . Cyprian in favour of believers' baptism" and Menno Simons "became acquainted with Cyprian's approval of adult baptism around 1529".[26] Conrad Grebel[27] wrote in 1524 to Thomas Münzer that

> the water does not confirm or increase faith as the scholars at Wittenberg say . . . also baptism does not save as Augustine, Tertullian, Theophylact and Cyprian have taught, dishonouring faith and the suffering of Christ. . . . Infant baptism is . . . contrary to all scripture, contrary even to the papacy; since we find from Cyprian and Augustine that for many years after apostolic times believers and unbelievers (i.e. *adults* from both Christian and pagan homes) were baptized together for 600 years.

If Cyprian was in many ways too much of an ecclesiastic to win the approval of left-wing Reformers, none the less Calvin, whose church-manship was staunchly of the Latin type, turned frequently to the Bishop of Carthage for support. He quotes even more often from Augustine, but Cyprian was a favourite Father at Geneva and citations are so numerous, especially in the fourth book of the *Institutes*, that only a summary can be attempted here.

One of Calvin's first public appearances as a Reformer took place at the Disputation of Lausanne in 1536, when he intervened with a re-markable *tour de force* by his extemporaneous quotation of many patristic references against Christ's corporeal presence in the eucharist. He began by saying that no Christian should neglect or despise the teaching of these great doctors of the church, and his appeal to Cyprian[28] took the following form:

> Even Saint Cyprian, when speaking of the present subject with which we are now concerned, in the second book of his letters, letter III (i.e. *Ep.* 63, 14),

does not wish that we should pay any regard to what our predecessors may have said or done, but that we should only consider the words of our master Christ who is before all.

On the subject of the sacrament Calvin frequently[29] appealed to Cyprian in support of communion in both kinds. If he, like Augustine, also approved of infant communion, that custom has now "deservedly fallen into disuse . . . the Supper is given to older persons who, having passed tender infancy, can now take solid food".[30] But for adults and especially for those approaching martyrdom the strength and consolation of the eucharist is profound. No Christian should be afraid of death; and Calvin says,[31] "I would advise such timid minds to read Cyprian's treatise *On the Mortality*, unless they deserve to be sent off to the philosophers."

But Calvin's chief appeal to Cyprian concerns the equality of bishops and the rejection of a papal primacy.

> For Cyprian, when he urges Stephen to warn the bishops of Gaul, does not base his argument upon fuller power but upon the authority that bishops have in common. I ask, if Stephen had then been in charge of Gaul, would not Cyprian have said, Compel them as they are yours? But he spoke far otherwise. "The brotherly fellowship", he says, "by which we are bound together among ourselves requires that we admonish one another." And we see also with what very harsh words this man of otherwise gentle disposition inveighs against Stephen himself when he thinks he has grown too haughty.[32]

He objected to Stephen's arrogance or ignorance, and always called Cornelius brother, fellow-bishop and colleague, in glaring contrast to "the very title of primate and other proud titles with which the Romanists wonderfully vaunt themselves".[33] Calvin conveniently forgets the papal title "servant of the servants of God", and continues his polemic against "this great insolence" of the papacy by quoting[34] Cyprian's remark as president of the African council that "none of us says he is the bishop of bishops". He had previously[35] cited the Textus Receptus of *De unitate* chapter four:

> What if I reply with Cyprian and Augustine that Christ did not (give the promise to Peter) to prefer one man to the others, but that he might so commend unity to the church? For so speaks Cyprian: In the person of one man the Lord gave the keys to all; the rest was the same as Peter was, endowed with an equal share both of honour and of power; but the beginning arose from unity that the church may be shown to be one.

In consequence Calvin claims[36] that he has only "to place before your

66

eyes the ancient form of the church as their writings prove it to have been in the ages of Chrysostom and Basil among the Greeks and of Cyprian, Ambrose and Augustine among the Latins, and after so doing to contemplate the ruins of that church which now survive among yourselves'', in order to prove that the difference between the papal and the ancient church is as great as that which the Old Testament prophets describe between the days of David and Solomon and the corruption under Zedekiah and Jehoiachin.

One feature of the early church which appealed to Calvin was the popular election of its bishops; he was by no means a radical democrat, but he thought that people as well as clergy should have an adequate share in appointing pastors. "While this rule was in force the church was in a state of good order," he writes,[37] after remarking that Cyprian regarded such a practice as having divine sanction. Neighbouring bishops according to Cyprian were present at elections to "act as moderators, lest any disturbance arise in the crowd",[38] but his writings also show that "in ancient times no one was even received into the assembly of the clergy without the consent of all the people".[39]

Another early practice applauded by Calvin was the exercise of church discipline in public.

> The public and solemn acknowledgment (exomologesis, as Cyprian calls it), which penitents were in ancient days obliged to make when they were to be reconciled to the church, no sane man does not commend and willingly adopt, provided it be not diverted to some other end than that for which it was instituted.[40]

> When these had been performed to the satisfaction of the church, the penitent was received into grace with laying on of hands, a reception that Cyprian often calls "peace". He also briefly describes such a rite. "They do penance", he says, "for a set period; then they come to public confession and through the laying on of hands of bishop and clergy receive the right to communion." Although the bishop with his clergy possessed a power of reconciliation, it required at the same time the consent of the people, as Cyprian elsewhere shows.[41]

On the one hand, Calvin quotes Cyprian[42] to the effect that, although sins committed in ignorance are largely excusable, "they who stubbornly reject the truth offered them by God's goodness have nothing to plead as an excuse"; on the other, he applauds the leniency shown by Cyprian[43] when he wrote, "Let a man mercifully correct what he can, let him patiently bear what he cannot correct, and groan and sorrow over it with love." In particular, he contrasts the severity of papal discipline with Cyprian's permission[44] for consecrated virgins to marry if they must. Such moderation is inevitable while the church contains tares as well as wheat, although it should not be made a pretext for schism or disorder, and, "Cyprian has put it well, Even though there seem to be tares or unclean vessels in the church, there is no reason why we ourselves should withdraw from the church."[45]

It is above all as an apostle of unity that Calvin praises Cyprian. And the means to unity are provided by fraternal fellowship and conciliar government at every level of church life.

> This power, as we have declared, was not in one man's possession to do whatever he pleased, but in the hands of the assembly of the elders, which was to the church what the senate is to the city. Cyprian, when he mentions those through whom the power was exercised in his day, usually associates the entire clergy with the bishop. But in another passage he also shows the clergy as so governing that the people were not excluded from deliberation. For he writes as follows: From the beginning of my episcopate I determined not to do anything without the advice of the clergy and the consent of the people.[46]

Jerome (*Ep.* 125, 15) discussed unity without mentioning the Pope, doubtless because he found the true basis of unity to be "what Cyprian most beautifully described in these words, 'The episcopate is one, a whole of which a part is held by each bishop. . . . The Bride of Christ cannot be an adulteress. . . .' You see that he makes the universal bishopric Christ's alone, who takes the whole church under himself."[47] In thus deriving the source of catholic unity "from Christ's episcopate alone"[48] Calvin claims that Cyprian was following St. Paul:

> We see how he continually calls us back to the Head himself (and) accordingly Cyprian declares that heresies and schisms arise because men return not to the Source of truth, seek not the Head, keep not the teaching of the heavenly Master.

Since scripture says, "Hear him . . ." we "must listen to Christ alone";[49]

> for what else does that statement of Cyprian mean which Augustine so often repeats, "We ought to glory in nothing because nothing is ours," except that man, rendered utterly destitute in his own right, should learn to depend wholly upon God?[50]

If the authority of God the Father is supreme for every Christian, God's church is the only mother through whom he can be born into new life. Calvin does not actually quote Cyprian on the church's motherhood, but the concept was held as dear in Geneva as it had been at Carthage.

> Because it is now our intention to discuss the visible (*sic*) church, let us learn even from the simple title "mother" how useful, indeed how necessary, it is that we should know her. For there is no other way to enter into life, unless this mother conceive us in her womb, give us birth, nourish us at her breast, and lastly unless she keep us under her care and guidance until, having put off mortal flesh, we become like the angels. . . . Furthermore, away from her bosom one cannot hope for any forgiveness of sins or any salvation.[51]

> The church is the common mother of all the godly, which bears, nourishes and brings up children to God, kings and peasants alike; and this is done by the ministry.[52]

If Calvin was on occasion stern and forbidding, there were times when the Christianity of Cyprian and Augustine equally deserved these epithets; but behind the apparent severity of all three authors there lay the passionate tenderness of love.

Meanwhile another section of mother church was setting her affairs in order at Trent, and here too Cyprian played a distinguished role among the patristic authorities that were quoted. Augustine, Jerome, Chrysostom and some other Fathers were mentioned with greater frequency, but Cyprian made his appearance not only in the formal proceedings but also from time to time in sermons that were preached before the council. At Ascensiontide, 1551, Dr. Peter Fragus maintained the validity of baptism in the blood of martyrdom, and in his printed text[53] there are marginal references to Cyprian along with Ambrose, Augustine and Bernard. The Dominican Henry de S. Hieronymo, preaching in Lent 1562 on the church's calamities, named Cyprian no less than six times[54] in connexion with moral questions, against the sins of pride and avarice, and on the necessity of remaining within the church. In January, 1563, on the Feast of the Circumcision, Robert Furnierus[55] quoted Cyprian Lib. II, Ep. 8 (i.e. *Ep.* 52) to prove that heresy is a punishment for impure and criminous living. Other sermons have about eight marginal references to the genuine Cyprian, and four to spurious Cyprianic writings, on points of doctrine, especially on church, sacraments and unity. Ludovic Villetanus,[56] disputing in 1562 on communion under the one species of bread, referred in his margin to Cyprian's *De lapsis* for judgement inflicted on unworthy communicants, and interpreted the narrative to imply that bread alone had been reserved. On the Feast of St. John the Apostle, 1562, Gaspar Ferrantius[57] quoted the *De unitate* and an epistle to Cornelius to prove that "Christ willed his church and flock to be shown as one" and that "we are with our head who is the Roman Pontiff, the vicar of Christ and successor of Peter". In Lent, 1563, Christopher Sanctotisius[58] preached from Cyprian to the effect that "no man can truly call God Father if he declines to receive the church as mother", and in a so-to-speak posthumous sermon, attributed to 1574 and certainly preached after the closure of the council, Peter Fontidonius[59] addressed the Germans in defence of Trent, asking,

> Whence have all these commotions, tumults, heresies arisen unless it is because, as that famous African pastor and martyr said, obedience is not shown to the priest of God?

The council itself, in Session XIV (1551), cap. 7 *On Reserved Cases*, referred to Cyprian along with Origen, Innocent III, Alexander III and others for the ruling that serious sins are only to be absolved by the "chief priests" (*a summis dumtaxat sacerdotibus*).[60] Session XXII (1562), cap. 7 *On Mixing Water with the Wine* quoted Cyprian's sixty-third epistle for the mixed chalice.[61] And Session XXIII (1563), cap. 1 *On the Institution of the Priesthood of the New Law* gave Cyprian (Lib. I, adv. Iudaeos, i.e. *Testimonia* I) as its only patristic authority for transformation of the Jewish priesthood into a visible and outward *sacerdotium* with the visible sacrifice of the eucharist.[62]

Considerable excitement was caused in 1563 when Manutius published the Primacy Text of Cyprian's *De unitate* for the first time; previous printings, such as the *editio princeps* of Cyprian (1471, Rome), had used the Textus Receptus of the work. A minor scandal lay behind the appearance of this edition, because the expert scholar Latino Latini refused to let his name be associated with it and believed the Textus Receptus to be alone authentic. But later catholic editions were based on PT, while protestants on the whole maintained that it was spurious, citing the TR version as it appeared in Gratian's *Decretum* and demonstrating Cyprian's opposition to papalism from his letters.

This controversy had an immediate bearing on current theological debate, because the closing sessions of Trent were much concerned with the relation of bishops to the Pope.[63] The question at issue was whether the episcopate had been instituted directly by Christ, or derived its power mediately through the Roman Pontiff; and in consequence whether it was divine or canon law which obliged a bishop to reside within his diocese. The latter question was put to the vote on April 20, 1562, when sixty-seven voted in favour of a divine obligation, thirty-eight allowed a canonical power of dispensing from the duty of residence, and thirty-four wished the matter to be referred to the Pope's judgement.

During the following October decrees and canons of the Sacrament of Orders were debated, with frequent appeal to Cyprian from both sides. Thus the Archbishop of Granada, arguing that the Pope would be the church's only bishop *iure divino* if others did not derive their power from Christ by direct institution, cited Cyprian's contention that "the episcopate is one, part of which is held in totality by each". Other speakers affirmed from Cyprian that the Pope's jurisdiction is ministerial but not dictatorial, and that all of the apostles had an equal authority with Peter. This apostolic equality was used to refute arguments based on Cyprian's acceptance of the Petrine commission to feed Christ's sheep.

On November 28, the Bishop of Città di Castella, claiming that Peter's primacy referred only to the origin of church unity, offered an interpretation of the phrase *in solidum*: this must imply at least two persons who hold in different ways, since only one at a time can own *in solidum* under Roman law, and thus it includes both the Pope's plenitude of power and the bishops' share in government (*pars sollicitudinis*). If all the apostles were equal, as understood from Cyprian's *De unitate*, the conclusion was drawn by the Bishop of Pamplona that all bishops alike have their position by divine right.

On May 12, 1563, the Cardinal of Lorraine tempered his insistence on the church's need of a single head by admitting that the episcopate must equally be one. Papal protagonists such as the Bishop of Cava distinguished order from jurisdiction, confining episcopal equality to that of order, and maintaining that although Christ himself instituted the apostolate, bishops receive their jurisdiction mediately through the Pope.

And on December 7, the Abbot-General of the Cistercians appealed to Cyprian's abhorrence of schism, declaring that unity must be sought under a papal supremacy alone. It was during this debate that news reached Trent of the publication by Manutius of PT; attempts were made to silence Latini's criticism; but the council made no attempt to define the relation between bishops and the Pope.

Among leading Roman Catholic theologians of the post-Tridentine period, Bellarmine[64] made a particular effort to exculpate Cyprian from the Donatism of Hussite and Anabaptist sects.

> It was thirteen hundred years ago that in Asia and Africa a mistaken doctrine began to appear, to the effect that sacraments are not valid if ministered by heretics and schismatics after their separation from catholic unity . . . (Augustine *De baptismo* II, 7) shows that the first author of this mistake was Agrippinus . . . the predecessor of S. Cyprian . . . (who) followed his predecessor's view along with many African bishops, but yet in such a way that he did not separate on this account from the unity of the church.

Bellarmine adds a pious hope, based on Augustine's forty-eighth epistle, that Cyprian may have recanted his error when moved by the authority of Pope Stephen; and he points out more plausibly that Cyprian did not anticipate the Donatists by impugning validity on grounds of the minister's unworthiness, but only on those of heresy or schism.

The Church of England was much influenced by continental Reformers during the sixteenth century but it desired, or was at least compelled by law, to retain much medieval practice in liturgy and order. Occupying a middle position between catholic and protestant, Anglicans naturally found the appeal to Cyprian acceptable. He himself would probably have regarded the Church of England as too nearly Donatist in its national isolation, but there is some historical basis for calling him the *Doctor Anglicus*. Von Soden[65] remarks that he could not have hoped to become the favourite author of an Elizabeth of England, but his Latin text none the less provided a staple part of her tuition under Roger Ascham, and his *Discipline of Virgins* "must have tested the endurance of this lively daughter of Henry VIII".[66] The Index Volume[67] to the Parker Society's edition of the Anglican Reformers has a sizeable list of entries under the name of Cyprian; and although these are not nearly as numerous as those under Augustine, the difference in bulk between the two authors' writings must be borne in mind.

Whitaker[68] quotes Cyprian in defence of the sole sufficiency of scripture; so-called tradition must be found in Gospels, Acts or Epistles if it is not to be rejected, and "Christ only should be heard". Cranmer[69] uses the same authority to prove that "neither ought we to follow the custom of man but the truth of God", while Jewel[70] tells his opponent Dr. Cole to "remember St. Cyprian's words that be alleged in your own decrees, Christ did not say I am custom but I am Truth". Jewel also has a lively passage-at-arms with Father Thomas Harding:[71]

72

We are bound to hear the church, said M. Harding. But much more are we bound to hear God. This saying of St. Cyprian is worthy deeply to be noted. A man is not joined to the church if he separates from the Gospel.

The church's motherhood is not often mentioned by English divines, but Fulke[72] says that when Cyprian referred to "the *matrix* and root of the catholic church" he was only warning travellers not to join a sect and was not, as Sanders had contended in his *Rock of the Church*, designating the Holy Roman Church by this expression. However if "mother church" is not explicitly mentioned—and I have only traced two[73] references, which is surprising in view of the constant study of Calvin by many Anglicans—there is none the less much on the subject of church unity. Jewel[74] explained this as a unity of one flock under many pastors with one bishopric diffused in mutual concord, adding the acid comment, "if either the author of the Apology or the interpreter understood not St. Cyprian, yet M. Harding, ye may give St. Cyprian leave to understand himself". Fulke[75] expounded Cyprian thus:

> The rest of the Apostles were even the same thing that Peter was . . . but the beginning proceedeth from one, that the church might be shewed to be one . . . the church, which is one, is founded by our Lord's voice upon one . . . thus far Cyprian, by which we see that there is but one beginning, yet all the Apostles are equal.

And the cause which Cyprian assigned for schism was accepted by several Anglicans,[76] when they found it in disobedience to the single bishop.

Church government should, however, be exercised by bishops in association with clergy and people (had Anglicans accepted this, much of the English dissent need not have occurred);

> Both elders and deacons, as saith Cyprian, and certain also of the common people were called thereunto.[77]

Cyprian was even quoted[78] as a moderate defender of presbyterian rights, since "for a consistory of elders is the word *presbyterium* used in Latin by Cyprian". But in opposition to Cartwright, Whitgift[79] insisted that bishops succeed to the apostles:

> I told you before that that part of the apostles' office which consisted in government is now remaining in archbishops and bishops. . . . Cyprian writeth thus, But deacons must remember that the Lord hath chosen apostles, that is to say bishops and chief governors.

For Anglicans the important point was to emphasize the equality and solidarity of the episcopate, and Fulke[80] interpreted the phrase *in solidum* to mean "the Bishop's office is one, whereof every man doth partake the Bishop's office wholly".

Archdeacon Philpot[81] was questioned about this at his remarkably courteous examination before the Marian clergy. Dr. Saverson remarked, "St. Cyprian . . . doth allow the bishop of Rome to be supreme head of the church." Philpot replied, "That I am sure of he doth not; for he writing unto Cornelius, then bishop of Rome, calleth him but his companion and fellow-bishop." When Saverson demurred, Philpot offered a wager, and when the text of Cyprian had been brought he cited *Ep. 59, 5*; Saverson tried to interpret this of the Roman supremacy, but Philpot answered that there were four Patriarchs, among whom Rome was "placed lowest in the council", and that each had a "college of learned priests, in hearing of whom by a convocation of all his fellow-bishops, with the consent of the people, all heresies were determined by the Word of God, and this is the meaning of St. Cyprian". A chaplain interrupted, "Did not Christ build his church upon Peter? St. Cyprian saith so," to which Philpot countered by remarking, "St. Cyprian *De simplicitate praelatorum* (i.e. *De unitate*) declareth in what respect he so said: God gave in the person of one man the keys of all, that he might signify the unity of all men." (It is obvious that Philpot is here quoting Calvin, with slight verbal changes due to lapse of memory.)

Whitgift similarly affirmed the equal status of all bishops, declaring that "the bishop of Rome had no jurisdiction over the bishop of Carthage",[82] and Jewel makes many references to Cyprian[83] in order to prove that, since the church is one, each congregation should have only one bishop, who is the Vicar of Christ in his own see. Although it was normal in the early church for the people to elect their bishop, Whitgift[34] opposing Cartwright maintained that this practice was not universal, that Cyprian occasionally failed to observe it, and that its purpose was merely to detect if the candidate had any faults. And Pilkington[85] defended the Anglican Ordinal against an anonymous Romanist:

> I proved afore by Paul and Timothy, by Dionysius etc. that the order, by which our bishops and priests are made now, is more agreeing to the order of the church in Cyprian's time, and tradition of the apostles, than that misorder whereby the popish prelates order their clergy.

The crux of the matter lay in the Petrine primacy, and before his martyrdom in 1555, Philpot[86] was again examined on this point:

A Doctor: What will you say if I can prove that Christ builded his church upon Peter, and that out of St. Cyprian? Will you then believe that the bishop of Rome ought to be supreme head of the church?

Philpot: I know what St. Cyprian writeth in that behalf; but he meaneth nothing as you take it.

A Doctor: St. Cyprian hath these words, That upon Peter was builded the church, as upon the first beginning of unity.

Philpot: He declareth that in an example, that unity must be in the church; he grounded on Peter his church alone, and not upon men. The which he doth more manifestly declare in the book *De simplicitate praelatorum,* saying In the person of one man God gave the keys to all, that he, in signification thereby, might declare the unity of all men.

A Doctor: What! Will you understand St. Cyprian so? That were good indeed.

Philpot: I think you cannot understand St. Cyprian better than he doth declare himself.

At this we read that Bishop Bonner handed over the examination to the Chancellor of Lichfield Cathedral, since he himself felt an urgent desire to attend Parliament.

Hooper[87] quoted the letters of Cyprian, Jerome and Augustine to prove that the title of pope was then "a general name to all bishops". Fulke[88] made an ingenious but implausible emendation to the text of Cyprian when he suggested that *Petrum* might be changed into *petram* so that the one church and chair would be founded by the Lord's voice on rock:

> Cyprian acknowledgeth no inequality of the Apostles . . . also that the building of the church upon one, and the receiving of the keys of one, was not an ordinary office to descend by succession, but a singular privilege for that one time, to shew the beginning and not the continuance of the power to proceed from one, but to be held always of One, which is Jesus Christ.

The same author[89] pointed out that in the case of the Spanish appeal, a papal sentence had been "pronounced void" by Cyprian's council, that in dealing with Marcian of Arles Cyprian urged a lazy Pope to join in condemning him, and that on the question of rebaptism the Africans denied any papal prerogative. "If Cyprian had thought the Pope and Church of Rome could not err, he would never have maintained an opinion against them," writes Fulke, and with this rejection of papal infallibility Jewel[90] wholeheartedly agrees. When Parker[91] wrote to Heath and other deprived bishops in 1560, he asked:

> Reverend Sirs, consider how St. Peter claimed no subjection; which St.

Cyprian . . . saith, "Peter . . . when St. Paul after strove with him, did not take upon him nor challenge anything insolently or arrogantly, neither advanced he himself as chief." . . . Because ye be so earnest with us of the Reformed Church . . . for subjection to foreign tribunals . . . pray, sirs, resolve us what tribunals did St. Cyprian and the eighty bishops of Carthage (*sic*) acknowledge when he said *Christus unus et solus habet potestatem de actu nostro iudicandi* (Christ has the one and only power to judge our action.)

That there is no "bishop of bishops" was a principle accepted by Bullinger and Anglican divines.[92] It was also accepted by a puritan like Cartwright, who used it to deny the metropolitan jurisdiction of Canterbury and York; to which Whitgift[93] replied that Cyprian himself in practice acted as an archbishop, and that his words were not intended to countenance presbyterian "anarchy".

On liturgical matters also Cyprian was an authority, sometimes hostile, and always to be reckoned with. Bullinger, Calfhill, Whitaker and Whitgift[94] condemned his "unscriptural" practice of consecrating the water for baptism (though this was to be retained both in the Prayer Book and in the Westminster *Directory* for public worship), and of anointing the baptized with oil. But Ridley,[95] when discussing Holy Communion, accepted what he called "Cyprian's doctrine" that *with* the sacrament "is given to the godly and faithful the grace of Christ's body, that is, the food of life and immortality", and he also thought it in accordance with Cyprian's teaching to believe that, if the nature of a sacrament is not to be destroyed, "bread must needs still remain". Cranmer[96] on the other hand found Cyprian a troublesome author on the subject of eucharistic sacrifice:

> The cause why Cyprian and other old authors say that Christ made an oblation and offering of himself in his last Supper . . . was that there he ordained a perpetual memory of his death . . . as the water (in the mixed chalice) doth signify and represent the people, so doth the wine signify and represent Christ's blood, and the uniting of the water and wine together signifieth the uniting of Christian people unto Christ himself. . . . Cyprian spake of no gross and carnal eating with the mouth, but of an inward spiritual and pure eating with heart and mind.

Jewel[97] argued that since Cyprian compared Christ's sacrifice to that of Melchizedek (*Ep.* 63, 4), he cannot have taught a corporeal presence in the eucharist; the story in *De lapsis* of the unworthy communicant who was burnt when taking the reserved sacrament from a box, "as it sheweth the manner of keeping of the sacrament, so it seemeth to shew that God was offended with the same";[98] and when Cyprian in *Ep.* 12,

2 spoke of offering sacrifice for the martyrs, he cannot have meant that the Blessed Virgin and the saints were in purgatory, since "otherwise you would much enlarge the pope's dominion".[99]

The Reformers felt themselves on firmer ground when they[100] cited Cyprian in proof that only God can pardon, or pointed out [101] that when he refused to accept immediate absolution of apostates on the strength of testimonials from martyrs, Cyprian denied in advance the doctrine of the Treasury of Merit. Jewel and Calfhill[102] found him a useful ally in condemning the veneration of images; indeed the latter offered a very free translation of his *Quod idola dii non sint* (cap. 7) as follows:

> These wicked Spirits do lurk in Shrines, in Roods, in Crosses, in Images, and first of all pervert the Priests, which are easiest to be caught with bait of a little gain, then work they miracles.

But Cyprian's attitude to vestments proved a little more difficult to understand. At his martyrdom the *Acta Proconsularia*[103] described him as wearing a *linea* or linen tunic, a *dalmatica* or Dalmatian dress used by the upper classes, and *lacerna byrrus*, both of which words mean "cloak" although the latter sounds somewhat like "biretta". Bullinger had no antagonism to vestments, and on May 1, 1566, he wrote[104] to Humphrey and Sampson:

> Eusebius truly bears witness from the most ancient writers that the Apostle John at Ephesus wore on his forehead a *petalum* or pontifical plate; and Pontius the deacon relates of the martyr Cyprian that, when he was about to present his neck to the executioner, he first gave him his *birrus* and his dalmatic to the deacon and then stood forth wearing only his linen garment.

To this his correspondents replied[105] in July:

> The ancient fathers had their habits; but these were neither peculiar to bishops nor distinguished from those of the laity. The instances of St. John and Cyprian are peculiar.

Cartwright argued that if the "cap" was given to the executioner it must have been of a common pattern to be of any use, that the "upper garment" was given to the deacon simply as a token of goodwill, and that Cyprian would not have rendered himself conspicuous in time of persecution by wearing a distinctive dress. Whitgift[106] quotes these arguments of Cartwright, but merely comments that the names *birrus* and *dalmatica* show that these were not items of "common apparel" for ordinary men to wear.

And so we return, almost to the point where we started, with the garments worn by Cyprian on his way to martyrdom. The Roman Empire under which he suffered was on the whole beneficent and just. But Vladimir Soloviev[107] has pictured Anti-Christ as an apparently beneficent and highly intellectual dictator, who persuades mankind to sell its soul in return for the material pottage of social welfare; he is elected President of the United States of Europe, imposes universal peace, and allows the churches to meet in a World Council at Jerusalem, on condition that they acknowledge him as their sole protector and defender. Most accept, but several church leaders doubt the dictator's credentials, demanding a confession of his personal faith in Jesus Christ the Son of God. John the Elder, with his deep Russian spirituality, is the first to recognize the Anti-Christ; Pope Peter II excommunicates him; and protestant resistance is headed by the German professor Ernst Pauli. At once the dictator launches a persecution under which Peter and John meet sudden death. Professor Pauli leads the faithful remnant out into the wilderness, and there, "after the restoration to life of Pope Peter and the Elder John, in the darkness of the night on a high and lonely place, was accomplished the Union of Churches". It may be that the fires of persecution, similar to that which Cyprian endured, will be needed to forge afresh for the body of Christendom that unity in love which he so ardently desired.

SELECT BIBLIOGRAPHY

THE ONLY COMPLETE critical edition of the Latin text of Cyprian is that by Wilhelm Hartel (*Corpus Scriptorum Ecclesiasticorum Latinorum*, vol. III, Vienna 1868–1871), which is defective and for which a replacement is much to be desired. Maurice Bévenot has used his extensive knowledge of the manuscripts to edit the *De unitate* in *The Tradition of Manuscripts* (1961); there is an earlier edition of the same treatise by E. H. Blakeney (1928), and it with other works has also been edited by J. N. Bakhuizen van den Brink (*S. Caecilii Cyprianii . . . scripta quaedam*, The Hague, 1946); yet another edition of Cyprian's treatises appears in S. Colombo, *Corona Patrum Salesiana*, series Latina II (Tübingen, 1935). The letters have been edited, with a translation into French, by Louis Bayard (2 vols., Paris, 1945–61).

An English translation of the whole appears in the *Ante-Nicene Christian Library*, vols. 8 and 13, by R. E. Wallis (1868–69), where the letters are given a different enumeration from that which is now standard; a comparative table of the numbers used in various editions will be found in Hartel, *op. cit.*, pp. cxix–cxxi. Bévenot has translated the *De lapsis* and the *De unitate* with annotations in *Ancient Christian Writers*, vol. 25 (1957). The *De opere et eleemosynis* is translated with a commentary by E. V. Rebenack (Washington, 1962), and Mary L. Hannan has done the same for the *De mortalitate* (Washington, 1933). Mention should also be made of T. A. Lacey, *Select Epistles of St Cyprian* (1922); S. L. Greenslade (ed.), *Early Latin Theology* (Library of Christian Classics, vol. 5, 1956—*De unitate* and two letters); Sister M. George Edward Conway, translation with commentary of *De bono patientiae* (Washington, 1957); and Roy J. Deferrari and others, translation of the treatises (New York, 1958).

Much of the literature on Cyprian is in French and German, with some in Italian, Dutch and Swedish; reference to this will be found in my footnotes, but for the convenience of the general reader, the select bibliography is here confined to works in English, and it does not include editions or translations mentioned in the previous paragraphs.

BENSON, E. W., *Cyprian, His Life, His Times, His Work* (1897).

BÉVENOT, M., *St. Cyprian's De unitate chapter 4 in the light of the manuscripts* (1939).

"A new Cyprian Fragment" in *Bulletin of the John Rylands Library* 28 (1944), 76–82.

"A Bishop is Responsible to God Alone" in *Recherches de Science Religieuse* 39 (Paris, 1951), 397–415.

"St. Cyprian and the Papacy, Musings on an Old Problem" in *Dublin Review* 228 (1954), 161–168 and 307–315.

"Primatus Petro Datur" in *Journal of Theological Studies*, new series 5 (1954), 19–35.

"Hi qui sacrificaverunt, a significant variant in St. Cyprian's De Unitate", *ibid.*, 68–72.

"In solidum and St. Cyprian, a correction", *ibid.*, 6 (1955), 244–248.

"The Sacrament of Penance and St. Cyprian's De lapsis" in *Theological Studies* 16 (1955), 175–213.

"St. Cyprian, a multi-centenary" in *The Month* 20 (1958), 159–166.

BUTLER, E. C., "St. Cyprian on the Church" in *Downside Review* 71 (1953), 1–13, 119–134 and 258–272.

CHAPMAN, J., "The order of the Treatises and Letters in the MSS of St. Cyprian" in *Journal of Theological Studies* 4 (1903), 103–123.

"The Interpolations in St. Cyprian's De Unitate Ecclesiae", *ibid.*, 5 (1904), 634–636.

"Professor Hugo Koch on St. Cyprian" in *Revue Bénédictine* 27 (Maredsous, 1910), 447–464.

DALY, C. B., "Absolution and Satisfaction in St. Cyprian's Theology of Penance" in *Studia Patristica* 2 (Berlin, 1957), 202–07.

EHRHARDT, A., "Cyprian, the Father of Western Christianity" in *Church Quarterly Review* 133 (1942), 178–196.

FREND, W. H. C., *The Donatist Church* (1952).

JALLAND, T. G., *The Church and the Papacy* (1942).

LACEY, T. A., *Unity and Schism* (1917).

MASCALL, E. L., "Collegiality, Reunion and Reform" in *Theology* 69 (1966), 201–208.

PLUMPE, J. C., *Mater Ecclesia* (Washington, 1943).

SWETE, H. B. (ed.), *Essays on the Early History of Church and Ministry* (1918).

SYKES, N., *Man as Churchman* (1960).

TURNER, C. H., "Prolegomena to the Testimonia and Ad Fortunatum of St. Cyprian" in *Journal of Theological Studies* 31 (1930), 225–246.

WATSON, E. W., *The Style and Language of St. Cyprian* (1896).
"The Interpolations in St. Cyprian's De Unitate Ecclesiae" in *Journal of Theological Studies* 5 (1904), 432–436.
WILES, M. F., "The Theological Legacy of St. Cyprian" in *Journal of Ecclesiastical History* 14 (1963), 139–149.
WILLIS, G. G., *St. Augustine and the Donatist Controversy* (1950).

NOTES

I

CYPRIAN'S BACKGROUND

1. "Nutricula causidicorum Africa", Juvenal *Sat.* vii, 148.

2. E. W. Benson, *Cyprian* (1897) 3.

3. For what follows cf. W. H. C. Frend, *Martyrdom and Persecution in the Early Church* (1965), 361–362.

4. "Linea, dalmatica, lacerna byrrus", *Acta Proconsularia* 5 (*Cypriani Opera*, ed. Guilelmus Hartel, C.S.E.L., Vienna 1871, III, iii, p. cxiii).

5. Cyprian, *Epp.* 39, 5 and 40 (Hartel 585); cf. P. Monceaux, *Histoire littéraire de l'Afrique Chrétienne* II (1902), 15.

6. *Acta Proconsularia* 1 (Hartel cxi).

7. Monceaux, *op. cit.* 7, lists the number of bishops attending Cyprian's councils and suggests a total of about 100; A. d'Alès, *La Théologie de Saint Cyprien* (1922), cites 129 in his appendix IV; von Soden, *Die Prosopographie des Africanischen Episcopats zur Zeit Cyprians* 20, reckons on at least 150.

8. *Epp.* 8, 30, 31, 36.

9. Cyprian organized his programme of Christian Aid with the words "respondere nos decet natalibus nostris", Pontius, *Vita Cypriani* 9 (Hartel c).

10. Cyprian, *Ep.* 27, 3 (Hartel 542).

11. "Qui et Thascius" in the superscription of *Ep.* 66 (Hartel 726); "Thascius Cyprianus" in *Acta Proconsularia* 3–4 (Hartel cxii–cxiii). Thascius was a popular nickname (cf. Pontius, *Vita* 15, Hartel cvii; Monceaux, II, 202). His proper name was turned by enemies into the abusive epithet of "Coprianus" (Lactantius, *Inst. Div.* V, 1). Jerome (*De viris illustr.* 67) says that he adopted the cognomen of the presbyter who converted him, but this was "Caecilianus" according to the MSS of Pontius, *Vita* 4, and Jerome's guess is probably an error (Benson 1, note 3). Cyprian's formal name, quoted from an official document in *Ep.* 66, 4 (Hartel 729), was Caecilius Cyprianus.

12. L. Bayard, *Saint Cyprien, Correspondance* I (1945), p. ix, suggests a date around 200 A.D. for his birth and 245 for his conversion; Monceaux, II, 203, would make him ten years younger, on the ground that he does not appear to have known Tertullian personally (but there is no reason why, in his pagan youth, he should have done so).

13. Pontius, *Vita* 15; Jerome, *loc. cit.*; Lactantius, *Inst. Div.* I, 24.

14. The influence of Seneca is noted in some of his writings by M. F. Wiles in *Journal of Ecclesiastical History* 14 (1963), 141.

15. Tradition came to describe him as a converted sorcerer. This began in the East, where Gregory of Nazianzus (*Oratio* 24, 8–12; P.G. 35, 1178–1184) confused him with his namesake Cyprian of Antioch; Prudentius (*Peristephanon* 13, 21–24; C.S.E.L. 61, 424) described him as "doctissimus artibus sinistris" with his "magicum cantamen" and in a poem attributed to Isidore of Seville (P.L. 83, 1254) he appeared as "ex mago sacerdos et martyr". Books of magic later circulated under his name, and the magician Cyprian became an ancestor of Faust (Monceaux II, 361); cf. J. Coman "Les deux Cypriens" in *Studia Patristica* IV, 1961, 363–372.

16. Pontius, *Vita* 2.

17. *Ad Donatum* 4 (Hartel 6).

18. Cf. *ad Donatum* (his earliest writing) *passim*.

19. *Ad Demetrianum* 3 (Hartel 352–353).

20. "Omnem substantiam suam" Jerome, *De viris illustr.* 67; but there is good MS evidence for reading "tota pro (i.e. prope) pretia", which implies that the sale was not complete.

21. *Epp.* 7 and 81 (Hartel 485, 841) *et al.*; "quantitas mea propria" may mean no more than the bishop's share of the general church revenues, but "horti nostri" are surely the residue of his personal estates.

22. Monceaux, II, 63.

23. *Sententiae Episcoporum* (Hartel 435–461).

24. S. L. Greenslade (ed.), *Early Latin Theology* (1956, Library of Christian Classics, vol. 5), 117.

25. L. Bayard, *Correspondance* I, ix; Monceaux, II, 205.

26. Benson, xxii; M. F. Wiles in *J.E.H.* 14, 140.

27. For the evidence, derived from *Epp.* 59, 6 and 29, see Benson 41, note 2.

28. On the chronology of Cyprian's writings see Benson, xxii–xxiii; Monceaux, II, 258; and for the epistles, L. Bayard, *Correspondance*.

29. *Ep.* 43, 4 (Hartel 593); for this aspect of Cyprian's character see J. Colson, *L'Evêque ... chez saint Cyprien* (Paris 1961) esp. 37 sq.

30. *Epp.* 11, 3 and 58, 1 (Hartel 497 and 656).

31. *Ep.* 66, 9–10 (Hartel 733–734).

32. *Ep.* 48, 4 (Hartel 608), quoted by O. Perler in Y. Congar & B.-D. Dupuy (ed.), *L'Episcopat et l'Englise Universelle* (1964), 51–52.

33. Benson 22 envisages an even earlier date, while Cyprian was still a presbyter, but the phrase "Quirino filio" (Hartel 35) suggests that he was already a bishop; however, the title of *Testimonia* III, 28 ("Non posse in ecclesia remitti ei qui in Deum deliquerit") implies that the Novatianist schism had not yet occurred (because it was in order to maintain this principle that Novatian separated from the church), and the treatise must therefore have been com-

pleted before the end of 250; cf. C. H. Turner in *Journal of Theological Studies* 31 (1930), 229–231.

34. J. Daniélou & H. Marrou, *The Christian Centuries* I (E.T. 1964), 196.

35. *Testim.* I, 16–17 (Hartel 49–51).

36. Jerome, *De viris illustr.* 53, tells us that he read Tertullian daily, calling for the volume with the phrase, "Da mihi magistrum"; but the master had died under the cloud of Montanism, and Cyprian never mentions him by name.

37. *De cath. eccl. unit.* 6 (Hartel 214); *De habitu virginum* 3 (189); *Epp.* 10, 1 and 4; 15, 2; 41, 2; 73, 19; 74, 7 (490, 494, 515, 588, 793, 804). The concept was shared by his correspondent Firmilian of Caesarea, *Ep.* 75, 14 (819).

38. J. N. Bakhuizen van den Brink in *Mededelingen der Koninklijke Nederlandse Akademie van Wetenschappen* N.R., 21 ix (Amsterdam, 1958), 254.

39. There are anticipations of the idea in Hermas (*Vis.* 3, 9. 1) and in "II Clement" 2, 1, but the earliest exact use of the title occurs in the letter of the Christians at Vienne and Lyons (Eusebius *H.E.*V, 1, 45 and 2, 7; cf. J. C. Plumpe *Mater Ecclesia*, Washington 1943, 36–37); Irenaeus is aware of the idea, and it is employed by Clement of Alexandria and Origen in allegorical exegesis (Plumpe 42, 63 *sq.*), but at Rome there is no direct use of it during the first three centuries (*ibid.* 126).

40. "Ne mater quidem Ecclesia praeteritur; si quidem in Filio et Patre mater recognoscitur, de qua constat et patris et filii nomen" (*De oratione* 2).

41. *De baptismo* 20.

42. *Ad martyras* 1.

43. "Sciebat illi sexum Mariae et deinceps ecclesiae profuturum" (*Adv. Marcionem* II, 4).

44. ". . . ut de iniuria perinde lateris eius vera mater viventium figuraretur ecclesia" (*De anima* 43); cf. *De monogamia* 5, where Christ has "one church as his spouse, according to the figure of Adam and Eve".

45. A collection of parallel passages is provided by L. Bayard, *Tertullien et Saint Cyprien* (Paris 1930); for a detailed comparison of Tertullian's *De oratione* with Cyprian's *De dominica oratione*, see Benson 276–279.

46. Cf. E. W. Watson in *Studia biblica et ecclesiastica* 4 (1896; "The Style and Language of St. Cyprian"), 197.

47. *De unitate* 12 (Hartel 220).

48. Hartel 26–27.

49. *Epp.* 71, 2 and 48, 3 (Hartel 772 and 607).

50. *De unitate* 23 (Hartel 231).

51. *Apologeticum* 21 (C.S.E.L. 69, 55–56).

52. *De praescr. heret.* 21 (C.S.E.L. 70, 25).

53. *De unitate* 6 (Hartel 215).

54. *Adv. Praxean* 8 (C.S.E.L. 47, 238–239), cf. 29 (*ibid.* 286) where the same metaphors are used to indicate a distinction of attributes in the one divine substance; this particular parallel with the writing of Cyprian has been noted by

J.-P. Brisson, *Autonomisme et Christianisme dans l'Afrique Romaine* (Paris 1958), 41.

55. *De unitate* 5 (Hartel 214).

56. *De praescr. heret.* 20 (C.S.E.L. 70, 24): omne genus ad originem suam censeatur necesse est. Itaque tot ac tantae ecclesiae, una est illa ab apostolis prima ex qua omnes. Sic omnes primae et apostolicae, dum una omnes. Probant unitatem communicatio pacis et appellatio fraternitatis et contesseratio hospitalitatis. Quae iura non alia ratio regit quam eiusdem sacramenti una traditio. See further P. Batiffol, *L'Eglise Naissante* (1927), 322.

57. *De baptismo* 15 (C.S.E.L. 20, 213-214).

58. *De praescr. heret.* 32.

59. "Locus" (τόπος) in *Adv. Haer.* I, 27, 1; III, 3, 1 etc.

60. *De praescr. heret.* 36.

61. *Ep.* 59, 14 (Hartel 683).

62. See the references collected by M. Maccarone in *Saeculum* 13 (1962), 283.

63. *De praescr. heret.* 36 (C.S.E.L. 70, 45-46).

64. *De monogamia* 8.

65. "An quia et petra et lapis Christus? . . . Itaque affectavit carissimo discipulorum de figuris suis peculiariter nomen communicare", *Adv. Marcionem* IV, 13, 5-6 (C.S.E.L. 47, 458).

66. *Scorpiace* 10, 8 (C.S.E.L. 20, 167): "memento claves eius hic dominum Petro et per eum ecclesiae reliquisse".

67. *Saeculum* 13 (1962), 281.

68. *De pudicitia* 21, 9-10 (C.S.E.L. 20, 269-71).

69. "Id est ad omnem ecclesiam Petri propinquam"; B. Poschmann *Ecclesia Principalis* (Breslau 1933), 7-8 proves that this must mean a church which derives its origin from Peter, and that the sense of geographical proximity, suggested by Harnack and Caspar, is in contradiction both with the context and with Tertullian's usage elsewhere.

70. Tertullian means that a plenary absolution can be granted in baptism, but the institutional church can bestow no forgiveness for post-baptismal sin.

71. "Principaliter"; this has the same meaning as "in principio" and it refers to temporal priority (cf. *De praescr. heret.* 31: "ad principalitatem veritatis et posteritatem mendacitatis").

72. *Comment. in Matt.* XII, 14 (P.G. 13, 1012-1013) and XII, 11 (*ibid.*, 1000).

73. H. von Campenhausen, *Kirchliches Amt und geistliche Vollmacht* (Tübingen, 1953), 292.

74. "Episcopatus aemulatio schismatum mater est" (Tertullian, *De baptismo* 17), cf. Cyprian, *Ep.* 59, 5 (Hartel 671-672) "neque enim aliunde haereses obortae sunt aut nata sunt schismata quam quando sacerdoti Dei non obtemperatur".

75. Tertullian, *De pudicitia* 1, 6 (whether this refers to a bishop of Rome or

of Carthage is immaterial for the present argument, but see H. Koch, *Cathedra Petri*, Giessen 1930, p. 6 and Poschmann, *Ecclesia Principalis* 10–11), cf. Cyprian, *Sentent. Episc.* (Hartel 436).

76. With Cyprian's thorough-going conciliarism compare Tertullian, *De paenitentia* 13, 6–7 (a catholic work): "aguntur praeterea per Graecias illa certis in locis concilia ex universis ecclesiis, per quae et altiora quaeque in commune tractantur, et ipsa repraesentatio totius nominis Christiani magna veneratione celebratur. Et hoc quam dignum fide auspicante congregari undique ad Christum. Vide, quam bonum et quam iucundum habitare fratres in unum" (I owe this reference to Hans Küng, *Structures of the Church*, E.T. 1965, p. 17).

77. *De praescr. heret.* 22.

78. *De pudicitia* 13.

79. *De praescr. heret.* 41.

80. *De oratione* 28 (C.S.E.L. 20, 198): "nos sumus veri adoratores et veri sacerdotes, qui spiritu orantes spiritu sacrificamus orationem hostiam Dei propriam et acceptabilem".

81. *De exhortatione castitatis* 7, cf. *De monogamia* 11–12.

82. *De baptismo* 17 (C.S.E.L. 20, 214): "summus sacerdos, qui est episcopus".

83. Clement of Rome describes Christ as the high priest (36) and appears (40) to use the title priest for bishops.

84. *De pudicitia* 22; in *Ad martyras* 1 the doubt is carefully and courteously concealed.

85. *De anima* 9 (written of course when the author was a Montanist).

86. See notes 30–32 above.

87. *De fuga in persecutione* 6.

88. *Ep.* 3, 3 (Hartel 471): "apostolos id est episcopos et praepositos".

89. *Scorpiace* 6 *et al.*

90. J. Colson, *L'Evêque . . . chez saint Cyprien* 113; see also the remarks o Perler in Congar-Dupuy, *L'Episcopat et l'Eglise Universelle* 45.

91. *Ep.* 81 (Hartel 841–842).

92. Died 259; see A. Ehrhardt in *Church Quarterly Review* 133 (1942), 180–181.

93. *De mortalitate* 26 (Hartel 313–314).

94. Cf. W. H. C. Frend, *The Donatist Church* (1952), 131: "It seems that the real measure of Cyprian's greatness is to be found in his own reconciliation of potentially rival conceptions of the church. His power was derived from an ability to combine the qualities of episcopacy with those of spiritual enthusiasm." This combination had been particularly notable in Ignatius of Antioch.

95. I owe the phrase, in another context, to my colleague Dr. T. O. Ling.

96. This is the main argument of Augustine *De baptismo contra Donastistas* II–VII.

97. *Cyprian*, preface p. ix.

II

THE PRIORITY OF PETER

1. *The Council and Reunion* (E.T. 1961), 194, 244, 251.

2. T. Granderath, ed. K. Kirch, *Geschichte des vatikanischen Konzils* III (1906), 448.

3. *Cyprian und der römische Primat* (Leipzig, 1910), 137.

4. O. Perler in Congar-Dupuy, *L'Episcopat et l'Eglise Universelle* (1964), 50.

5. *Structures of the Church* (E.T. 1965), 201; quoting G. Dejaifve in *Theologie und Glaube* 51 (1961), 2.

6. M. Bévenot in *Dublin Review* 228 (1954), 167–168.

7. Fulgentius of Ruspe, *De remissione peccatorum* I, 21 (P.L. 65, 544); see P.-Th. Camelot in *Istinia* 4 (1957), 433, note 16 and E. C. Butler in *Downside Review* 71 (1953), 258.

8. P. Monceaux, *Hist. litt. de l'Afrique Chrétienne* II (1902), 292.

9. *Ep.* 54, 4 (Hartel 623).

10. E. W. Benson, *Cyprian* (1897), 180.

11. Dom J. Chapman in *Revue Bénédictine* 20 (1903), 28–29; for the Roman envoys see *Ep.* 44 (Hartel 597–598).

12. H. Koch, *Cyprianische Untersuchungen* (Bonn, 1926), 107; *Cathedra Petri* (Giessen, 1930), 33; and E. Caspar, *Primatus Petri* (Weimar, 1927), 27 *sq.*

13. "Nemine episcopatum dante episcopi sibi nomen adsumunt", *De unit.* 10 (Hartel 218), cf. "uno in loco . . . multos pastores", *ibid.*, 8 (216); see Koch, *Cyprianische Untersuchungen* 88, who compares these with the language of *Epp.* 44 (597–599) and 69 (749 *sq.*) which are explicitly directed against Novatian.

14. M. Bévenot, *The Lapsed: The Unity of the Catholic Church* (1957, Ancient Christian Writers, vol. 25) 6; cf. S. L. Greenslade, *Early Latin Theology* (1956, Library of Christian Classics, vol. 5), 119–20.

15. *Revue Bénédictine* 63 (1953), 79–84.

15a. *Ep.* 15, 4 (Hartel 516) *et al.*

16. I have translated the Latin text as given by Bévenot in *The Tradition of Manuscripts: a study in the transmission of St. Cyprian's treatises* (1961), 99–101, the Roman numerals being derived from the same author's divisions in *Journal of Theological Studies* n.s. 5 (1954), 26–30; Hartel (212–214), prints TR alone.

17. *Cyprian* 203.

18. J. Chapman in *Revue Bénédictine* 19 (1902), 246–254 and 357–373; 20 (1903), 26–51; 27 (1910), 447–464.

19. A. Harnack, *Chronologie* II (1904), 364; J. Ernst, *Cyprian und das Papsttum* (1912), 10 *sq.*; A. d'Alès, *La Théologie de St. Cyprien* (1922), 104 *sq.*; E. Caspar, *Primatus Petri* (1927), 277 *sq.*; K. Adam, *Theologische Quartalschrift* (1928), 211 *sq.*

20. P. Batiffol, *L'Eglise naissante* (1909), 447; T. A. Lacey, *Unity and Schism* (1917), 168 *sq.*

21. See esp. *Cathedra Petri* (1930), 114–147.

22. E. W. Watson in *Journal of Theological Studies* (1904), 432 *sq.*; O. Casel, *Pastor Bonus* (1914), 312–314; J. H. Bernard in H. B. Swete (ed.), *Essays on the Early History of the Church and Ministry* (1918), 250–253.

23. In *Revue d'histoire ecclésiastique* 29 (Louvain, 1933), 5–24.

24. See the names listed by M. Bévenot in *Journal of Theological Studies* n.s.5 (1954), 20.

25. J. Ludwig, *Primatworte* (in *Neutestamentliche Abhandlungen* 19, 1952), 20–36.

26. J. le Moyne in *Revue Bénédictine* 63 (1953), 70–115; this article begins with a full and well-documented account of the various opinions.

27. M. Bévenot, *St. Cyprian's De unitate c. 4 in the light of the manuscripts* (1939), 36–39; see further in the same author's *The Tradition of Manuscripts* (1961).

28. Apart from its emphasis on the equality of the apostles, it denies (c. 11) the validity of schismatic baptism; no forger at the time of the Donatist controversy would have retained this denial.

29. Ludwig, *Primatworte* 33–34; Firmilian's letter appears as *Ep.* 75 in the Cyprianic corpus and its most relevant chapter is 17 (Hartel 821).

30. *Ibid.*, 24–25.

31. Bévenot in *Journal of Theological Studies* n.s.5 (1954), 27–29, makes too much of his alleged break in the sequence of thought between VII and the resumption of the common text, and his attempted reconstruction is unnecessarily involved, applying VI to Felicissimus and VII to Novatian.

32. In *Revue d'histoire ecclésiastique* 29 (1933), 12–19.

33. See van den Eynde, *op. cit.* 21–22 and Bévenot in *Journal of Theological Studies* n.s.5 (1954), 58–72.

34. This reading is confirmed by the second letter of Pelagius II to the bishops of Istria in 584/9 (E. Schwartz, *Acta Conciliorum Oecumenicorum* IV, ii, 111) which is two centuries older than the earliest manuscripts of Cyprian.

35. *De bono patientiae* 19 (Hartel 411), and *Ep.* 73, 25 (798).

36. *Testim.* II, 1 (Hartel 63); the *primatus* here ascribed to Christ is rendered in the English versions as pre-eminence or supremacy, but it is a translation of the Greek πρωτεύων which can mean first in time rather than rank, a meaning which is perhaps supported by the word "first-born" earlier in the same verse.

37. *Ep.* 69, 8 (757).

38. Such is the suggestion of le Moyne in *Revue Bénédictine* 63 (1953), 109, who sees in it the hint of a power greater than that possessed by others.

39. *Ep.* 71, 3 (773).

40. The point is illustrated by a series of quotations collected by Hugo Koch, *Cathedra Petri* 45.

41. *Ecclesia Principalis* 31–32.

42. *Ep.* 71, 3 (Hartel 773); the date of this letter is 255 (Bayard, Monceaux and Benson), or 256 (Rouet de Journel *Enchiridion Patristicum*, p. 210).

43. *Ep.* 73, 11 (786), date 256.

44. Hartel 210–211.

45. *Ep.* 59, 7 (674).

46. *De habitu virginum* 10 (194); this is one of Cyprian's earliest works, dated to 249 by Monceaux and by van den Eynde in *Revue d'histoire ecclésiastique* 29 (1933) 16; while Benson gives the date 248.

47. "Nam Petro primum Dominus, super quem aedificavit ecclesiam et unde unitatis originem instituit et ostendit, potestatem istam dedit ut id solveretur quod ille solvisset. Et post resurrectionem quidem ad apostolos. . . ." *Ep.* 73, 7 (783).

48. "Una ecclesia . . . super Petrum origine unitatis et ratione fundata." *Ep.* 70, 3 (769).

49. *Ep.* 33, 1 (566); the date is 250, before the composition of the *De unitate.*

50. *Journal of Theological Studies* n.s.5 (1954), 22, note 1.

51. *Contra Parmenianum* I, 10; in view of this, le Moyne is wrong in saying that Cyprian could not have used the phrase to describe an African schismatic, *Revue Bénédictine* 63 (1953), 92.

52. *Increpatio in clerum* (P.L. 69, 367): "Sedem Petri apostoli immundis pedibus aliquos usurpantes . . . Iudam quodam modo in Petri cathedram . . . statuunt"; T. A. Lacey, *Unity and Schism* 183, comments that "we may either trace in this the influence of St. Cyprian or find in it evidence that he was not altogether singular in his use of the phrase".

53. Cornelius was made bishop "cum Fabiani locus id est cum locus Petri et gradus cathedrae sacerdotalis vacaret", *Ep.* 55, 8 (630).

54. *Ep.* 59, 14 (683): "navigare audent et ad Petri cathedram atque ad ecclesiam principalem".

55. E.g. "noti atque . . . pro suis facinoribus exclusi" in the same *Ep.* 59, 16 (686); "de Dei voluntate atque omnium nostrum consensione", *Ep.* 55, 8 (630); "tractatu longo atque argumentis", *De unit.* 4 (212).

56. His letter appears among Cyprian's as *Ep.* 75, 17 (821–822).

57. *Ep.* 59, 14 (683).

58. Cyprian's succession list must have treated Peter as the first bishop of Rome, because he regards Hyginus as the ninth, cf. *Ep.* 74, 2 (801).

59. H. Koch, *Cathedra Petri* 95–102; his view is accepted by le Moyne, *Revue Bénédictine* 63 (1953), 113; and with qualifications by P.-Th. Camelot, *Istina* 4 431; but rejected by G. Bardy, *La Théologie de l'Eglise* II (1947), 239–240.

60. B. Poschmann, *Ecclesia Principalis* (Breslau, 1933) 63; cf. P. Batiffol, *Cathedra Petri* (1938), 135–150.

61. Cicero, *Rep.* VI, 25, 27, writes "hic fons, hoc principium est movendi, principii autem nulla est origo; nam e principio oriuntur omnia". E. C. Butler

in *Downside Review* 71 (1953), 267–268, notes the parallel between this and Cyprian's "ecclesia *principalis* unde . . . *exorta* est", cf. "unitas servatur in *origine*" (*De unit.* 5). Irenaeus *adv. Haer.* IV, 38, 3 has: "principalitatem habet in omnibus Deus quoniam et solus infectus et prior omnium". Tertullian can use the word to signify supreme authority (cf. Poschmann *op. cit.*, 48), but also temporal priority as in *De praescr. heret.* 31: "revertar ad principalitatem veritatis et posteritatem mendacitatis disputandam". See P. Batiffol, *L'Eglise naissante* 252.

62. *Cyprian* 538.

63. The earliest statement found by Koch (*Cathedra Petri* 86–89) to the effect that Rome is the mother of all churches dates from 462 A.D. and is made by Leontius of Arles, *Ep.* 5, 1.

64. *Ep.* 48, 3 (607), ". . . communicationem tuam id est catholicae ecclesiae unitatem".

65. *Ep.* 55, 1 (624), ". . . te secum hoc est cum catholica ecclesia communicare".

66. *Cathedra Petri* 72.

67. S.v. "Cyprian" in *Catholic Encyclopedia* IV, 588.

68. See *Ep.* 68, esp. sections 1, 3 and 5 (744, 745 and 748–749).

69. See further Chapman in *Revue Bénédictine* 27 (1910), 459, note 2.

70. *Ep.* 67 (735 *sq.*).

71. *Cyprian* 234.

72. Cf. Vincent of Lerinum *Commonit.* 1, 6; Augustine *De baptismo contra Donat.* III, i, 3; xii, 17 *et al.*

73. *Ep.* 75, 7 (815).

74. *Ep.* 73, 23 (796).

75. *Sententiae Episcoporum* (Hartel 435–461).

76. *Ibid.*, 436.

77. Cf. Bévenot in *Journal of Theological Studies* n.s.5 (1954), 34–35, and in *Dublin Review* 228 (1954), 307–315.

III

THE COLLEGIALITY OF BISHOPS

1. *Sentent. Episc. praef.* (Hartel 436), cf. *Ep.* 66, 3 (728).

2. Poschmann, *Ecclesia Principalis* 90, note 124, thinks that he was; for the contrary view see Bévenot in *Recherches de Science Religieuse* 39 (1951), 413.

3. *Op. cit.*, 397–415.

4. Their letter appears as *Ep.* 30 (549 *sq.*) in the corpus of Cyprian's correspondence; his own previous communication to them is *Ep.* 20 (527 *sq.*).

5. In *Ep.* 36, 4 (575) the Roman clergy praise him for informing them of a local African scandal; in *Ep.* 59, 9 (676) he apologizes to Cornelius for not writing more quickly about the appointment of a schismatic bishop.

6. See *Ep.* 55, 21 (639); it is obvious that he was using Novatian's letter because in section 5 (627) he quotes an entire sentence from it.

7. *Epp.* 57, 5 (655) and 59, 14 (683).

8. *Epp.* 69, 17 (765–766, where Rom. 14: 12–13 is quoted in support); 72, 3 (778); 73, 26 (798, where it is said that each bishop has the freedom of his own judgement); and *Sentent.Episc.* praef.(436, where this freedom of private judgement is combined with inability to judge or be judged by others). For a less pointed expression see *Ep.* 74, 8 (805).

9. *Ep.* 64, 1 (717).

10. *Ep.* 3, 1 (469).

11. Cf. E. C. Butler in *Downside Review* 71 (1953) 8, "the fact is that a bishop's right to rule his flock depends on that recognition by his fellow-bishops in the universal church which *communicatio* involves".

12. T. A. Lacey, *Unity and Schism* (1917), 98–99, who refers further to T. M. Lindsay, *Church and Ministry in the Early Centuries* (1902). This provides an interesting example of agreement between an Anglo-Catholic and a Scottish Presbyterian.

13. Cf. M. F. Wiles in *Journal of Ecclesiastical History* 14 (1963), 143–144.

14. See A. Beck, *Römisches Recht bei Tertullian und Cyprian* (Halle, 1930), 156–164.

15. *Ep.* 67, 4 (738).

16. *Epp.* 65, 2 (723); 67, 1 (736); 72, 2 (777).

17. *Epp.* 3, 1 (469); 4, 4 (476); 43, 7 (596); 59, 4 (670); 66, 3 (728).

18. *Ep. ad Corinth.* 40–44.

19. *Ep.* 33, 1 (566): "quando ecclesia in episcopo et clero et omnibus stantibus sit constituta". The "stantes" are the opposite of the lapsed, this term being "identical with, if not borrowed from, the gladiatorial name for the victor" (E. W. Watson, *The Style and Language of St. Cyprian* 292).

20. H. von Campenhausen, *Kirchliches Amt und geistliche Vollmacht* (Tübingen, 1953), 306–307.

21. Readers in *Ep.* 38, 2 (580); exorcists in *Ep.* 23 (536); acolytes in *Epp.* 7 (485) and 34, 4 (570); subdeacons in *Epp.* 29 (548) and 34, 4 (570); and deacons, presbyters and bishops *passim*.

22. See the epistle of Cornelius ap. Eusebius *H.E.* VI, 43, 11.

23. *Ep.* 5, 2 (479).

24. *Ep.* 7 (485).

25. *Ep.* 29 (548).

26. See *Ep.* 30, 5 (553) where the Roman clergy tell Cyprian that they must postpone a decision because they have no bishop to "moderate" ("qui omnia ista moderetur") since the martyrdom of Fabian.

27. See the superscriptions of *Epp.* 5 (478) and 27 (540).

28. *Ep.* 18, 1 (524).

29. *Ep.* 3, 3 (471).

30. *Ep.* 5, 2 (479).

31. See *Ep.* 34, 4 (570–571).

32. *Epp.* 69, 8 (757) and 73, 9 (785); the latter passage describes the rite of confirmation, "which now is performed among us also, so that those who are baptized in church are presented to the church's prelates, and through our prayer and the imposition of hands they obtain the Holy Spirit and are perfected with dominical consignation".

33. "Episcopum in ecclesia et ecclesiam in episcopo", *Ep.* 46, 8 (733).

34. *Ep.* 73, 11 (786).

35. *Ep.* 9, 1 (489).

36. *De lapsis* 6 (240–241).

37. *Ep.* 67, 1 (735).

38. *Ep.* 59, 17 (687).

39. *Ep.* 81 (841), written in 258 shortly before Cyprian's own martyrdom.

40. *Testim.* I, 16 (49–50), "That the old sacrifice should be abolished and a new one celebrated," and I, 17 (50–51), "That the old priesthood should cease and a new priest come who should abide for ever."

41. J. B. Lightfoot, *Philippians* (1868), 258; this dissertation on the ministry is also published separately. Lightfoot is wrong in ascribing a Gentile origin to Cyprian's sacerdotalism; traces of it appear in Christian tradition from the first century onwards, and Jewish prototypes are always quoted.

42. Cf. M. F. Wiles in *Journal of Ecclesiastical History* 14 (1963), 144.

43. See T. M. Lindsay, *Church and Ministry in the Early Centuries* 307–310.

44. A. Harnack, *History of Dogma* (E.T. 1900), II, 136.

45. *Ep.* 63, 17 (714).

46. E. W. Watson, *The Style and Language of St. Cyprian* 258, note 1; he only lists five instances where *sacerdos* could possibly mean a presbyter.

47. *Ep.* 61, 3 (697).

48. *Ep.* 55, 1 (624).

49. *Ep.* 55, 8 (629).

50. In *Ep.* 75, 21 (823).

51. *Ep.* 73, 23 (796); both these epistles belong to the year 256.

52. *Ep.* 64, 2 and 4 (718–20).

53. *Ep.* 72, 1 (775).

54. I *Apol.* 66.

55. M. F. Wiles in *Journal of Ecclesiastical History* 14 (1963), 148.

56. Harnack, *History of Dogma* II, 136, note 2.

57. Cf. Ignatius, *ad Rom.* 6, "permit me to imitate the passion of my God" and Polycarp's prayer (*Martyrdom* 14) before his martyrdom with its language reminiscent of the liturgy.

58. *Ep.* 63, 17 (714); the following sentences are taken from the same epistle, sections 1, 9 and 14 (701, 708 and 713).

59. *Ep.* 15, 1 (514), cf. 17, 2 (522).

60. *Ep.* 63, 13 (711–12); the simile of many grains making one loaf is found in *Didache* 9; the comparison of water/wine to people/Christ is first made by Cyprian, although the mixed chalice is mentioned by Justin (I *Apol.* 65), Irenaeus (*adv. Haer.* IV, 33, 2 and V, 2, 3) and Clement of Alexandria (*Paedagogus* II, 2, 20).

61. *Ep.* 58, 1 (657).

62. *Ep.* 5, 2 (479).

63. *Ep.* 39, 3 (583).

64. *Ep.* 1, 2 (466).

65. *De opere et eleemosynis* 15 (384).

66. *De lapsis* 25–26 (255–56).

67. *Ep.* 3, 3 (471).

68. *Ep.* 43, 1 (591); cf. J. Colson, *L'Evêque* (Paris, 1961), 51.

69. *Ep.* 4, 4 (476–77).

70. J. H. Bernard in H. B. Swete (ed.), *Early History of Church and Ministry* (1918), 229.

71. T. A. Lacey, *Unity and Schism*, 189–90.

72. *Ep.* 67, 3 (738).

73. J. H. Bernard, *op. cit.*, 232.

74. *Ep.* 45, 3 (602), "unitatem a Domino et per apostolos nobis successoribus traditam"; cf. *Ep.* 66, 4 (729), ". . . Christi qui dicit ad apostolos ac per hoc ad omnes praepositos qui apostolis vicaria ordinatione succedunt, Qui audit vos me audit"; and *Ep.* 3, 3 (471), "apostolos id est episcopos et praepositos".

75. *Ep.* 74, 10 (808).

76. *Ep.* 69, 3 (752).

77. S. L. Greenslade, *Early Latin Theology*, 120.

78. *Ep.* 43, 1 (591).

79. *Ep.* 67, 5 (739).

80. *Ep.* 45, 3 (602).

81. *Ep.* 55, 8 (629–30).

82. *Ep.* 59, 5 (672).

83. *Ep.* 61, 3 (696).

84. *Ep.* 46, 1 (604).

85. Ap. Eusebius, *H.E.*VI, 43, 11.

86. *Ep.* 41, 1 (587).

87. G. Klein, "Die hermeneutische Struktur des Kirchengedankens bei Cyprian," in *Zeitschrift für Kirchengeschichte* 68 (1957), 57–59. The references to Cyprian's letters are 66, 8 (733); 55, 21 (639); and 43, 5 (595).

88. J. Colson, *L'Evêque* 15.

89. T. Strotmann, O.S.B., in Congar-Dupuy, *L'Episcopat et l'Eglise Universelle* (1964), 322.

90. See P.-Th. Camelot, O.P., "St. Cyprien et la Primauté" in *Istina* 4 (1957), 424–429; for a diagram of the structure of this unity, descending from Christ through Peter and the apostles to the collective episcopate, consult A. Palmquist, "Kyrkaus Enhet och Papalismen" in *Acta Universitatis Upsaliensis* 1 (Upsala, 1961), 20, who stresses (*ibid.*, 15–16) that Cyprian's concern for unity was practical and not idealistic, arising out of the incidence of persecution and schism; and for a summary of its practical operation in church life, reference may be made to the table of contents in J. Colson, *L'Evêque* (Paris, 1961), 117–118.

91. *Ep. 66*, 8 (733).

92. *Ep. 68*, 4 (747).

93. *Ep. 68*, 5 (748).

94. *Ep. 36*, 4 (575).

95. *Epp. 48*, 1 and 2 (606); 14, 4 (512); 45, 2 (601).

96. *Epp. 18*, 1 (523); 19, 1 (525); 20, 1 (527).

97. *Ep. 38*, 1 (579).

98. In *Ep. 49*, 2 (610).

99. R. Sohm, *Kirchenrecht* I, 247–343; summarized in T. M. Lindsay, *Church and Ministry in the Early Centuries*, 327–334.

100. Cf. esp. Cyprian, *Ep. 55*, 5 (627), quoting a letter of the Roman clergy, to the effect that the treatment of the lapsed should be decided by taking common counsel with bishops, presbyters, deacons, confessors and also the faithful laity.

101. *Ep. 17*, 3 (523).

102. *Ep. 19*, 2 (526).

103. *Sentent. Episc.* praef. (435).

104. *Ep. 66*, 8–9 (733–34). Written in 254 to a schismatic confessor named Florentius Puppianus.

105. *De unit.* 5 (214).

106. E. W. Benson, *Cyprian* 182; cf. J. H. Bernard in Swete's *Early History of Church and Ministry* 244.

107. T. A. Lacey, *Unity and Schism* 35.

108. E. H. Blakeney, *Cyprian De Unitate Ecclesiae* (1928), 62; quoting C. Bigg, *Origins of Christianity* (1909), 363.

109. H. Koch, *Cyprian und das römische Primat* 28.

110. O. Casel in *Revue Bénédictine* (1913), 418; see further B. Poschmann, *Ecclesia Principalis* (1933), 19.

111. G. Bardy, *La Théologie de l'Eglise* (1947), II, 201.

112. J. le Moyne in *Revue Bénédictine* 63 (1953), 106.

113. S. L. Greenslade, *Early Latin Theology* (1956), 127, note 12.

114. M. Bévenot in *Journal of Theological Studies* n.s.6 (1955), 244–248.

115. In *Digest*. 45, 2, 3.
116. J. le Moyne *loc. cit.*
117. In *Digest*. 13, 6, 5 and 15 etc.
118. *Inst.* 4, 6, 36.
119. In *Digest*. 41, 2, 1 and 7.
120. *Op. cit.*, 247.
121. E. L. Mascall in *Theology* LXIX, no. 551 (1966), 206; he refers further to J. Mayendorff, *The Primacy of Peter* 28.

IV

THE CHURCH AND THE CHURCHES

1. *Ep.* 4, 4 (477); *De mortalitate* 6 (300), etc. See E. W. Watson's entries in *The Style and Language of St. Cyprian*.
2. *Ep.* 74, 6–7 (804), thrice.
3. *De unit.* 6 (214), etc.
4. *Ep.* 55, 5 (627), "ecclesiis omnibus"; contrast Cornelius in *Ep.* 49, 2 (611), "there should be one bishop in a catholic church".
5. *Epp.* 10, 1 (490); 10, 4 (494); 15, 2 (515); 41, 2 (588); 73, 19 (793); 74, 7 (804).
6. *De habitu virginum* 3 (189).
7. *De lapsis* 9 (243).
8. *De unit.* 6 (214).
9. The allegory was to become a favourite one in the Latin middle ages, by which time Noah had been identified with the Pope; Tertullian (*De idol.* 24, *De bapt.* 8) had used it in the same way as Cyprian.
10. *Ep.* 48, 3 (607).
11. *Ep.* 74, 11 (809); the scriptural reference is 1 Pet. 3: 20–21.
12. "Unitatis sacramentum"; the phrase is also found in *De unit.* 4 and 7 (213 and 215); *Epp.* 45, 1 (600); 69, 6 (754); 73, 11 (786); 75, 14 (820). The last of these letters is by Firmilian.
13. Cf. *De unit.* 6 (215).
14. J.-P. Brisson, *Autonomisme et Christianisme dans l'Afrique Romaine* (Paris, 1958), 43, 59 etc.
15. *Ep.* 43, 5 (594).
16. *Ep.* 70, 3 (769).
17. P.-Th. Camelot, O.P., "Saint Cyprien et la Primauté" in *Istina* 4 (1957), 422–423.
18. *Ep.* 55, 24 (642).
19. A. Harnack, *History of Dogma* (E.T. 1900), II, 85, note 1.
20. *Ep.* 74, 11 (808–09).

21. T. G. Jalland, *The Church and the Papacy* (1944), 164, note 3.

22. *Ep.* 74, 2 (800).

23. *Ad Fortunatum* praef. 3 (318).

24. All found in *Ep.* 69, 2 (750–51), and the second and third in *Ep.* 74, 11 (808–09).

25. *Ep.* 63, 14 (712).

26. *De unit.* 7 (215–16).

27. *Ep.* 69, 5 (754).

28. *Ep.* 55, 21 (639).

29. *Ep.* 43, 5 (594).

30. *De unit.* 8 (216–17).

31. *De unit.* 23 (231), "in solidam corporis unitatem", a phrase which recalls the tenure of the episcopate "in solidum" (*De unit.* 5); in *Ep.* 66, 8 (733) the bishops are the glue which holds the church together.

32. *De unit.* 27 (232).

33. *Ep.* 70, 1 (767–68), "neminem baptizari foris extra ecclesiam posse, cum sit baptisma unum in sancta ecclesia constitutum". This is the reason for the Presbyterian dislike of baptism by lay people.

34. *Ep.* 70, 2 (768); cf. G. G. Willis, *St. Augustine and the Donatist Controversy* (1950), 97, for the African creed.

35. *Ep.* 16, 2 (519).

36. C. B. Daly, "Absolution and Satisfaction in St. Cyprian's Theology of Penance" in *Studia Patristica* II (Berlin, 1957), 202 *sq.*, where further references are given.

37. Cf. the case of Bishop Therapius in *Ep.* 64, 1 (717).

38. *Epp.* 15, 3 (515); 21, 2–3 (530–31); 37, 4 (578); *De lapsis* 17–18 (249–50) and 36 (263).

39. *Ep.* 55, 18 and 29 (636 and 647).

40. B. Capelle in *Recherches de théologie ancienne et médiévale* 7 (1935), 224 *sq.*

41. *Testimonia* III, 28 (142); quoting Matt. 12: 32; Mark 3: 28 *sq.*; I Sam. 2: 25.

42. *De lapsis* 17 (249).

43. *Ep.* 73, 21 (795) written to Jubaianus in 256: "salus extra ecclesiam non est".

44. *Ep.* 55, 24 (642).

45. *De unit.* 11 (219).

46. *Ep.* 43, 4 (593).

47. *Ep.* 44, 1 (597).

48. *Ep.* 65, 2 (723).

49. *Ibid.*, 3 (724).

50. *De unit.* 21 (229).

51. *Ibid.*, 19 (227); cf. *Epp.* 55, 17 (636) and 73, 21 (794–95); referring to I Cor. 13: 3.

52. *De unit.* 14 (222–23).

53. *Ibid.*, 6 (215).

54. *Testimonia* III, 86 (174); quoting Eccl. 10: 9; Exod. 12: 46; Ps. 133: 1; Matt. 12: 30; 1 Cor. 1: 10; Ps. 68: 6 (references to the Psalms are here given according to the English versions).

55. *De unit.* 12 (220).

56. *Ibid.* (220–21).

57. *Ibid.*, 18 (226).

58. *Ep.* 69, 8 (756–57).

59. *Testimonia* I, 22 (57–58); quoting Isa. 65: 13 and 15 *sq.*, 5: 26 *sq.* and 3: 1; Ps. 34: 8 *sq.*; John 6: 35, 7: 37 *sq.*, and 6: 53.

60. *De unit.* 3 (211–12).

61. *Ibid.*, 13 (221–22).

62. *Ibid.*, 17 (225–26).

63. *Ibid.*, 9–10 (218).

64. *Ep.* 59, 5 (671–72).

65. *Ep.* 3, 3 (471–72).

66. E. W. Benson, *Cyprian* 230; referring to *Ep.* 55, 11 (632).

67. Cf. *Ep.* 72, 2 (776).

68. Benson, *op. cit.*, 137; but on p. 153 Benson corrects the theory of O. Ritschl (*Cyprian von Karthago und die Verfassung der Kirche*, 1885, I, 57–65) that Cyprian used his personal fortune as a relief fund in order to secure a following by bribery, and that the presbyters of Carthage prompted Felicissimus to resist this scheme.

69. There are no grounds for assuming that he ordained Felicissimus to the diaconate; his offence lay in appropriating a deacon without the bishop's knowledge; cf. *Ep.* 52, 2 (618) and see Benson, *op. cit.*, 115–116 and P. Monceaux, *Hist. litt. de l'Afrique Chrétienne* II, 31.

70. Ap. Eusebius, *H.E.* VI, 43.

71. *Ep.* 55, 24 (642–43).

72. *Ep.* 43, 5 (594–95).

73. *Ep.* 52, 1 (617), quoting Eph. 5: 31–32.

74. *De baptismo libri septem* esp. II, i, 2; vii, 12; V, vii, 8; VI, i, 1 (C.S.E.L. 51, 174–176, 186, 269 and 297–298).

75. II, 44 (18), *ibid.*, 376.

76. *Ep.* 54, 3 (622–23).

77. G. G. Willis, *St. Augustine and the Donatist Controversy*, 102.

78. E. W. Benson, *Cyprian*, 191.

79. *Ad. Smyrn.* 8, 2, "Wherever the bishop appears there let the people be, just as wherever Christ Jesus is, there is the catholic church."

80. Cf. Cornelius ap. Eusebius, *H.E.* VI, 43, 11, "there should be one bishop in a catholic church".

81. *Ep.* 51, 1–2 (614–15), cf. P. Batiffol, *L'Eglise naissante* 427

82. E. C. Butler in *Downside Review* 71 (1953), 2; M. Bévenot (transl.), *St. Cyprian, The Lapsed: The Unity of the Catholic Church*, 74–75.

83. H. Koch, *Cathedra Petri*, 63.

84. E. C. Butler, *op. cit.*, 6.

85. R. Sohm, *Kirchenrecht* I, 247–343.

86. Cf. Cyprian's, *Sentent. Episc.* praef. (435).

87. *Ep.* 55, 6 (627).

88. H. Küng, *Structures of the Church*, 31.

89. E. W. Benson, *Cyprian*, 157.

90. "La grande riunione del popolo christiano" (H. Küng, *op. cit.*, 23).

91. E. C. Butler, *op. cit.*, 13.

92. M. Bévenot, *op. cit.*, 5.

93. *Ibid.*, 10.

94. P. Batiffol, *L'Eglise naissante*, 455–457; cf. the same author's *Cathedra Petri*, 11.

95. See pp. 30–31 above.

96. See p. 30 above.

97. J. Chapman in *Revue Bénédictine* 27 (1910), 461.

98. For these comments, cf. M. F. Wiles in *Journal of Ecclesiastical History* 14 (1963), 139–142.

99. G. G. Willis, *St. Augustine and the Donatist Controversy*, 103.

100. S. L. Greenslade, *Early Latin Theology*, 116.

101. See pp. 55–56 above.

102. A. Beck, *Römisches Recht bei Tertullian und Cyprian* (Halle, 1930), 149.

103. *De unit.* 14 (223).

v

THE APPEAL TO CYPRIAN AT THE REFORMATION

1. *Hist. Eccl. Centuriae* (I quote throughout from the Basel edition of 1624), III, cap. x, 169–175.

2. III, cap. iv, 58.

3. III, cap. vii, 110–118.

4. *Annales Ecclesiastici*, vol. II; I quote from the Antwerp edition of 1597.

5. 412.

6. 423.

7. 431.

8. 435.

9. 464–65.

10. 478, quoting the conflated version of PT with TR.

11. 519.

12. 521.

13. 523.

14. 527.

15. 528.

16. N. Sykes, *Man as Churchman* (1960), 43–44; with reference to Luther, *Omnia Opera* I, 244a, 246b, 247a, 250b and 331a.

17. H. J. Hillerbrand, *The Reformation in its own Words* (1964), 67 *sq.*; from the Weimar Ausgabe II, 279 *sq.*

18. Weimar Ausgabe II, 405.

19. *Ibid.*, X, ii, 144.

20. 4–5 (Hartel 299).

21. Heb. 2: 14, in Weimar Ausgabe, LVII, part 3 (English translation by J. Atkinson, *Luther, Early Theological Works*, 1962, Library of Christian Classics, vol. 16, 62).

22. Weimar Ausgabe VI, 506.

23. *De unit.* 17, *sub. fin.* (226).

24. G. H. Williams and A. M. Mergal, *Spiritual and Anabaptist Writers* (1957, Library of Christian Classics, vol. 25), 148.

25. See G. H. Williams, *The Radical Reformation* (1962), 187.

26. *Ibid.*, 317 and 389.

27. Williams and Mergal, *op. cit.*, 80–81.

28. *Calvini Opera* IX (Corpus Reformatorum 37), 877 *sq.*; French text in B. J. Kidd, *Documents of the Continental Reformation* (1911), 551; English translation by J. K. S. Reid, *Calvin, Theological Treatises* (1954, Library of Christian Classics, vol. 22), 39–40.

29. *Institutes*, Prefatory Address to King Francis 4 (English translation by F. L. Battles in Library of Christian Classics, vol. 20, p. 21; this two-volume translation concludes with a most valuable index) and Book IV, 17, 49 (L.C.C. 21, 1427); cf. *Dilucida Explicatio* of the Lord's Supper against Heshusius (1561) translated by J. K. S. Reid, *op. cit.*, 299, "Cyprian contends that the blood of Christ is not to be denied to believers who are called to the service of Christ and obliged to shed their own blood."

30. *Inst.* IV, 16, 30 (L.C.C. 21, 1352); the reference to Cyprian is *De lapsis* 9 and 25 (Hartel 243 and 255).

31. *Inst.* III, 9, 5 (L.C.C. 20, 717); cf. the similar quotation by Luther in note 21 above.

32. *Inst.* IV, 7, 7 (1126).

33. IV, 7, 3 (1121).

34. IV, 7, 21 (1140).

35. IV, 6, 4 (1106).

36. *Reply to Cardinal Sadoleto* (1539), transl. Reid, *op. cit.*, 231.

37. *Necessity of Reforming the Church* (1543), trans. Reid, 207.

38. *Inst.* IV, 4, 14 (1083).

39. IV, 4, 10 (1078).

40. *Necessity of Reforming the Church*, trans. Reid, 216.

41. *Inst.* IV, 12, 6 (1235, with footnote references to *Epp.* 57; 16, 2; 17, 2; 14, 4; see Hartel 650 *sq.*, 518, 522, 512).

42. *Inst.* Pref. to King Francis 5 (23–24); the references to Cyprian are *Epp.* 63, 17 and 73, 13 (Hartel 715 and 787).

43. IV, 12, 11 (1239); Calvin paraphrases Cyprian, *Ep.* 59, 16 (686) in the light of Augustine, *contra Epist. Parmeniani* III, 1, 2.

44. *Ep.* 4, 2 (474) cited in *Inst.* IV, 13, 17 (1272).

45. *Inst.* IV, 1, 19 (1033); cf. *Ep.* 54, 3 (622 *sq.*).

46. IV, 11, 6 (1217–18); cf. *Epp.* 16, 2; 17, 2; 14, 4 (518, 522, 512).

47. IV, 6, 17 (1117); cf. *De unit.* 5–6 (214).

48. IV, 2, 6 (1047).

49. *Inst.* Pref. to King Francis 4 (22); cf. *Ep.* 63, 14 (712).

50. II, 2, 9 (266); cf. *Testimonia* III, 4 (116) and Augustine, *De praedestinatione sanctorum* 3 and 4.

51. IV, 1, 4 (1016).

52. *Comment. on Eph.* 4, 13 (quoted L.C.C. 1016, note 10).

53. Mansi, *Concilia* 33, 327.

54. *Ibid.*, 663 (twice), 665 (twice), 666 and 667.

55. *Ibid.*, 765.

56. *Ibid.*, 643.

57. *Ibid.*, 755.

58. *Ibid.*, 883.

59. *Ibid.*, 1061.

60. *Ibid.*, 96.

61. *Ibid.*, 130.

62. *Ibid.*, 138.

63. N. Sykes, *Man as Churchman*, 45–47; and for what follows on the Council of Trent, see the same volume 47–51, with references and quotations in the notes on 176–178.

64. *De controversiis Christianae Fidei* III (1619 edn.), 101–102 (i.e. De Sacramentis I, 26).

65. H. von Soden, *Die Cyprianische Briefsammlung* (Leipzig, 1904), 3.

66. J. Hurstfield, *Elizabeth I and the Unity of England* (1960), 7–8.

67. This lists a number of references to pseudo-Cyprianic writings: Ridley (Parker Society's edition 243), Latimer (II, 269) and Cranmer (I, 308) all quoted as Cyprian's the *De coena Domini* against transubstantiation, but this treatise is now attributed to the twelfth-century Arnold of Chartres; Cranmer (II, 23) quoted an exposition of the creed, which may be by Rufinus, against including the apocrypha in the canon of scripture; and both Pilkington (144) and Fulke (II, 234) confused Cyprian with Tertullian as author of the phrase "the blood of the martyrs is the seed of the church". These and all subsequent references to

the Anglican Reformers are made from the volumes of the Parker Society's edition.

68. Whitaker, *Disputation on Holy Scriptures*, Q. 6 (690–92); quoting *Epp.* 74, 2 and 63, 14 (Hartel 800 and 712).

69. Cranmer, *Confutation of Unwritten Verities*, cap. 7 (II, 50), quoting *Ep.* 63, 14 as above; cf. Becon (I, 376) and Pilkington (537).

70. Jewel, *Controversy with Dr. Cole* (I, 64).

71. Jewel, *Controversy with M. Harding of communion under both kinds* (I, 254), quoting *De lapsis* 16 (248); further quotation of the same passage by Jewel (II, 998; III, 223; IV, 876) and Sandys (94).

72. Fulke, *Discovery of the Dangerous Rock of the Popish Church* (II, 342), quoting *Ep.* 48, 3 (607).

73. Bradford (I, 503) and Bullinger (V, 90).

74. Jewel, *Defence of the Apology of the Church of England* (III, 300); quoting *De unit.* 5 (214); *De dominica oratione* 8 (271); *Epp.* 55, 24 (642); 66, 8 (733); and 68, 4 (747).

75. Fulke, *Discovery*, cap. 5 (II, 283, 290, 291); quoting *De unit.* 4 (213) and *Ep.* 73, 11 (786); cf. Jewel (I, 360; III, 201; and IV, 1136).

76. Fulke (II, 332); Jewel (I, 349; 373; and III, 605); and Whitaker (441).

77. Jewel (IV, 909).

78. Fulke, *Defence of the English Translations of the Bible* (I, 153).

79. Whitgift, *Defence of the Answer to the Admonition* viii (II, 355); quoting *Ep.* 3, 3 (471); cf. Whitaker (418), who quotes *Ep.* 75, 16 (821).

80. Fulke, *Discovery* (II, 316).

81. Philpot, 5th Examination (42–44).

82. Whitgift (II, 207; cf. 210–211).

83. Jewel, *Controversy with M. Harding* (I, 347, 348, 349, 385, 409, 434).

84. Whitgift, *Defence* iii (I, 358, 360, 362, 444).

85. Pilkington (605).

86. Philpot, 7th Examination (75–76).

87. Hooper, *Exposition on Ps. 23* (II, 236).

88. Fulke, *Discovery* (II, 334; cf. 290–291 and 331).

89. Fulke (II, 342–343 and 345; cf. his discussion of the term *principalis ecclesia* on 341).

90. Jewel (IV, 720–21).

91. Parker (110–11); cf. Cyprian, *Ep.* 71, 3 (773), and *Sentent, Episc.* (436).

92. Bullinger (IV, 110); Fulke (II, 322); Jewel (III, 300); Whitgift (II, 208).

93. Whitgift, *Defence* (II, 164, 192–221, 428).

94. Bullinger, 5th Decade, sermon 8 (IV, 363); Calfhill, *Answer to Martiall*, art. 4 (225); Whitaker, *Controversy* I, q. 6, cap. 12 (601–02); Whitgift, *Defence* (I, 217).

95. Ridley (201 and 175).

96. Cranmer, *Answer to Gardiner* iii (I, 86–87, 121, and 158).

97. Jewel, *Controversy* (II, 731, 762).

98. Jewel (I, 151).

99. Jewel (III, 561).

100. E.g. Becon, *Catechism* (II, 172).

101. Tyndale, *Answer to Sir Thomas More's Dialogue*, cap. 11 (III, 199).

102. Jewel (II, 645–646); Calfhill (317–318).

103. Hartel, cxiii.

104. *Zurich Letters* (I, 350–351).

105. *Ibid.*, 160.

106. Whitgift, *Defence* (II, 23–25).

107. See the summary of Soloviev's "Story of Anti-Christ", written near the close of his life in 1900, in N. Zernov, *Three Russian Prophets* (1944), 149–150.

INDEX